Black African Literature

BLACK AFRICAN LITERATURE
An Introduction

J. - P. Makouta - Mboukou

Black Orpheus Press
Washington, D.C.
1973

Translated by Alexandre Mboukou

CIP

Library of Congress Cataloging in Publication Data

Makouta-Mboukou, Jean Pierre, 1929–
Black African literature.

(Dimensions of the Black intellectual experience)
Translation of Introduction à la litterature noire.
1. African literature—History and criticism.
I. Title. II. Series.
PL8010.M313   809'.8967   76-172328
ISBN 0-87953-002-2

contents

BLACK AFRICAN LITERATURE

PART I:
forms

Is there such a thing as Black literature?
The issue of Black literature has indeed
generated a great deal of controversy.
Why speak of a Black African or a Black American
literature when nobody speaks of a White
literature?
First we must determine whether there is a black
race. The answer, here, is both immediate
and unequivocal.
In essence, does this black race enjoy the same
worldly status as the white race?
Here, too, the answer is both immediate and
unequivocal!
Well then, since we are all aware that there is
a black race which has known an economic
existence less enviable than that of the white
race in general; that is, as we are all aware
that the black race has been victim of a
historical accident, namely the imposition of
a humiliating status upon it by the so-called
civilized world, naturally we can understand
why this awareness has been accompanied by a
sigh, a moan, a cry of anxiety which has
expressed itself in a certain manner. And
when that expression is translated formally,
it is necessarily in a literary form.
Therefore, we should not be wondering whether
there is a Black African or Black American
literature. The fact is that whenever a people
has individuals who are ready to lend their
voices to the soul of the people in order to
give it expression, and make it become conscious

of its own existence, of its eternal values, of its past, or simply of its facilities for fighting for its survival, that people possesses a literature, even if its means of expression are only oral.

Whether in America or Africa, have Blacks not had thousands of opportunities to vent their indignation in many ways?

There has been from the beginning, of course, an oral folk literary expression of African society. All the wisdom of the Black world has been diffused in that literature, and it is to it that we must first turn.

CHAPTER 1:
folk literature

the african
oral tradition

We shall call this form folk literature to distinguish it from what we shall discuss later as elite literature. Unlike the written literature of modern times, folk literature was accessible in a certain measure to the whole African community: men, women, children, young people, adults, and the elderly.

Its forms were numerous: the best known are proverbs, folk tales, and songs.

Proverbs: Proverbs are the most poetic and the most carefully fashioned form of folk literature. They have a stable form and do not suffer from variations brought about by the whims of individuals.

The proverb existed before the individual person and it outlives him.

Moreover, proverbs are carriers, bearers of philosophical potentialities and of immutable inner meanings.

Because they are both precise and concise, proverbs impress, decide, convince; they settle arguments.

In fact the proverb is a very short literary form. It requires at times no more than a single word, the key word, the rest supposedly being known to all.

Let us take an example: *"Gong."* This means to be two-faced; to be *gong* is to have two different opinions on a given situation, depending on the people in whose presence they are expressed.

The proverb is the form most used in the traditional African court of justice where regular judicial contests occur. It used to happen, and it still happens occasionally, that an entire legal case would be argued solely in proverbs.

Today lawyers back their arguments by written texts, laws, and examples of previous judgments, but the traditional black judge or lawyer depends on his memory.

The most concise, the most polished form of thought, the proverb in principle requires age, reason, experience, and reflection.

That explains why this literary form is normally found in that part of society which is mature and accustomed to reflection. It also explains why this genre is threatened with extinction if it continues to be passed only by word of mouth. The traditional layer of the population which is the repository for it is disappearing, and this literary form runs the risk of disappearing with it.

Folk Tales: The folk tale is another traditional African literary genre. It is more readily accessible than the proverb.

Unlike the proverb, the folk tale does not have a fixed form. The storyteller can change it as he sees fit. What counts, of course, is the philosophy the tale expresses, the idea it contains.

Depending on the style of each storyteller, a story will be long or short. Some are short by nature; others are long, and they require a good and resourceful memory.

In the tales ideas are more fully developed and the narrator aims at two main goals: entertaining and teaching.

The tale pleases and entertains in a number of ways. Through its developed form, it allows the poet to embellish it to suit his fancy. Through its story—which is always an anecdote—the style of the narrator may be altered at will. Finally, through its sung parts, whether they are exhilarating or sad, the tale appeals to the soul; it is conceived, therefore, to please.

It is generally in the evening, by moonlight or in front of a big fire, that the storyteller shows off. The folk tale is therefore conceived of primarily as a pastime, a relaxation in the evening after a hot day of working in the sun.

In the process of entertaining, however, the folk tale educates and teaches by offering moral

precepts—for example, denunciation of the consequences of an irregular life, of some lie or slander,
of treason, of egotism, of infidelity, of stupidity, of
ambition, of stinginess, etc.

The folk tale may also instruct by developing a
paradox found in nature. For example:

> The gazelle is small but smart.
> The leopard is strong and brutal, but silly: it is
>   deceived easily.
> The monkey is an instinctive animal, but clever
>   and mischievous.
> Man is equipped with a conscience and reason;
>   however, he often lacks the presence of
>   mind to act accordingly; etc.

There is, therefore, always a lesson, implicit or
explicit, to be inferred from the tale. This lesson is
so extremely important that the narrator very often
presents the events as if they really had happened in
order to impress its moral on credulous children.

Thus in its double objective, to amuse and to
instruct, the folk tale is closely related to many
Western literary forms, including:

Drama: Certain folk tales are miniature theatri-
cal plays, with a setting, a subject, an introduction,
a climax, a denouement, and of course, characters.

Novel: Some tales are well developed, and present a theme in such a way that a whole lifetime is
unfolded; they are really novelettes or abridged
novels.

Poetry: The tale is usually a poem in blank
verse with its refrains, its repetitions, and the regular return of oratorical themes or rhythms.

All this led the late Langston Hughes, a great contemporary Black American poet to say, "The direct pleasure of reading [or of narration] is for me the first justification of literary creation." This is true for literary creation in general, and for black literary creation in particular.

Riddles: A riddle is a game in which the mind must guess the object or idea designated by a given sign, indication, or question.

The riddle game—which was popular in traditional African societies—develops the memory, imagination, thought processes, and judgment by associating signs with ideas, ideas with signs, ideas with ideas, and signs with signs.

In the long run, signs or indications become codified and end up by always designating the same ideas. Here are some examples from traditional Black Africa:

Sign, Question, or Indication	Solution
It always stares at the nose	a pipe
The house my father built has only one pillar	a mushroom
There is a deep forest from which no child's cry can be heard	pregnancy

African riddles are somewhat similar to proverbs in that they have an almost rigid form; the poet cannot embellish beyond a certain limit imposed by the length of the riddle itself. The riddle must, in fact, be brief; the answer is always a single idea often contained in a single word.

We sense in these riddles the following:
—A philosophy of everyday experience
—A commonsense philosophy
—A sense of elementary geometry
There is not, a priori, a moral to be drawn from this type of literature. It is designed first of all to amuse and to divert. Nevertheless, as we have suggested earlier, it has an enormous influence on the education and the development of the intellect.

Songs: Proverbs, folk tales, and riddles are traditional African art forms. It will never be known exactly when these forms originated. That their existence is common to all African societies is undisputed.

The talent of the African folk poet resides only in the practice of the art of his narrative that he embellishes in accord with his own poetic insight. He always works with an accepted traditional tale.

But songs are a poet's living construction. They are born in every epoch, following remarkable events. Songs, then, can be dated and pinpointed in time and space.

Proverbs, folk tales, and riddles have a universal value on the African scene, the same types recurring in almost identical fashion in all Black African societies. Songs, on the contrary, have only a local existence. They arise in a given region, at a given moment. And often they do not travel beyond the tribe, the district, the region, or the administrative division.

Traditional African songs always express a sentiment; they are in fact a way for the Black man to express his soul through music.

The song composer expresses honestly what he feels and what the people whose feelings he is expressing feel. In this the songs are different from modern songs, which do not always express a genuine experience. The modern composer writes songs to earn money, even if he doesn't believe what he says.

Traditional songs also convey a moral—a warning, ridicule, criticism, entreaty, flattery, thanks, abuse, defiance, a demand, repulsion.

Their moral lesson may be direct or may take an ironic form, often biting and caustic.

Songs are the common people's most lively literary form because they are constantly renewed.

Nevertheless, because they are tied to specific events, songs lose their flavor with loss of interest in the event. When there are new events, new songs arise spontaneously—song composers are plentiful. Moreover, this genre is still oral and runs the same risk of dying out as all oral literature.

The Oral Tradition and Written Literature: All this literature, which reaches every Black African social level, constitutes a powerful foundation of thought, an inexhaustible treasury of ideas, a more or less renewable means of expression, an aggregate of values not yet fully exploited by the African intellectual.

Proverbs, for example, could have given birth to poetic works comparable to La Rochefoucauld's *Maxims* or Pascal's *Pensées.*

Folk tales could have created African poets in the manner of a La Fontaine. Dramatists like Perrault could have put men and animals on the stage in enjoyable plays of African life.

Songs could have aroused songwriters able to measure up to such singers as Beranger.

But Black writers, called into action by a revolutionary cause, preferred to use more direct literary forms like poetry, the novel, and the political pamphlet. We hope that once this wave of demands and period of struggle is past, Africans will feel liberated and real poets will reemerge, poets who will make an examination of conscience and understand themselves more fully. They will be able to verify the wealth of their own heritage and make use of it to clothe the heart of their people in a new pride.

As a result of the short examination of traditional oral literature that we have just made, we can notice that an inborn creative genius exists among Black Africans which compares with that of other peoples of the world.

But for true literature to be born, that which will permit judgment of literary men, of novelists, and of poets, we must go beyond the oral, folk stage in order to move on to the period of written literature; we must therefore create conditions favorable to that literary production. In creating these conditions, we must consider the implications of the *problem of language*. In order for a literature to be born in a nation, the writers in that nation must have at their disposal a language which will allow them to express their moods and the views of the common people—the very soul of the nation. When that language is the mother tongue, expression is freer and more original. Unhappily for Black Africa, that condition has been only very partially fulfilled.

Many African poets, born poets, often do not know how to read or write. For the most part, colonialism brought the first rudiments of literary knowledge which allowed us to acquire the art of reading and writing.

With that possibility, Black African writers moved with no transition from the oral stage to the written stage. The new literature was unlike traditional African folk literature, which used to reach every social level, in that it reached only a small minority of people initiated in the languages in which that literature was expressed. The new African literature became a literature for the elite minority who had acquired knowledge of non-African languages.

CHAPTER 2:
elite literature

We call this *elite literature* because it is addressed only to the elites who know the languages in which that literature is expressed.

These elite languages are the languages of colonialization. The so-called colonialization languages were implanted by the colonial powers. These languages quite literally invaded Africa; their character varies in relation to the power of the colonizing country. This is how Africa came to be cut into pieces according to the number of European countries that colonized it or according to local linguistic predominance.

French-speaking Africa: West Africa, Equatorial Africa, Zaïre, Burundi, Rwanda. In these countries the colonial language is French.

English-speaking Africa: some of West Africa, East Africa, the Union of South Africa.

Arab-speaking Africa: includes all North Africa, Morocco, the northern half of Sudan, Mali, Chad, the northern part of the Central African Republic.

Portuguese Africa: Angola, Mozambique.

Spanish Africa: Fernando Po, Río de Oro, Equatorial Guinea.

Italian Africa: Eritrea.

Dutch Africa: the South African population of Dutch origin.

The black populations have had to and still have to learn these languages to understand what is expressed in them.

And the colonial powers did not allow everyone to become educated.

To this handicap is added the multiplicity of languages and of dialects spoken in Black Africa. Because of that, African writers opt to write in the language of colonization which predominates in their country, even though they can be appreciated only by those who speak the language of colonization. For the writer it is a question of thinking and reasoning in the language he is asking to carry his thought. Unfortunately, the African writer often restricts himself to speaking only the language of colonization, that is a language he has learned. But everyone knows that the merits of a people—moral, spiritual, and psychological are not readily transposed and find their truly appropriate expression only in the maternal tongue.

Langston Hughes was right in saying, "To communicate from one country to another, from one culture to another, especially when the language is not your mother tongue, but a language you have learned—that is, English and French for several of these writers—constitutes a great source of difficulty."

It is a problem for all prominent Black writers including:

Dahomean—Olympe Bhêly-Quénum

Senegalese—Léopold Senghor, Cheikh Hamidou Kane

Guinean—Camara Laye

Antillean—Aimé Césaire

Haitian—Jacques Roumain

Congolese—Tchikaya Utamsi, Jean Malonga

South African—Can Themba, Phillis N'Tanlala, Bloke Modisane, Peter Abrahams

Sierra Leonean—Abioseh Nicol

Ghanaian—J. Benibengor Blay, J. H. Kwabena Nketia.

Cameroonian—Mongo Beti, Ferdinand Oyono.

Despite the fact that all of these writers are animated by Black spiritual values, language constitutes a definite handicap. It is extremely difficult to be obliged to express one's soul in a language that is not one's own, whose unknown wiles and pretenses play blind man's bluff with one, and keep in store myriad surprises.

Nevertheless, it is in these foreign languages that our Black African writers express themselves. And so, we must pay our respect to them when they succeed, and offer sincere encouragement when they falter.

So much for the writer. But the Black African reader also has his difficulties. Certain African poets apparently believe that the more incomprehensible a poem is, the better it is appreciated; they withdraw like artistic hermits and venture forth no more.

And when you ask them what their art means, they answer, "There is nothing to understand, one must simply feel."

And of course, the common people, accustomed to simple oral folk literature, are unable to follow them. And this paradoxical situation results: the Black writer wants to show his soul to his people, but he winds up confining himself in a hermetic coffin in which he suffocates and from which he will issue forth only by accommodating himself to his people until they have the possibility of knowing how to read the mystery of the art of the muses.

New Directions for Black Literature: When will true Black literature be born? It will be born with the help of great events, which will overturn the hierarchical structures recognized until now. This great upheaval will awaken consciences and talents, for as Diderot says, "Poetry wishes for something enormous, barbaric, and wild."

And the question Diderot posed to himself can still be posed insofar as black literature is concerned: "When shall we see poets born?" he asked. His answer was as follows:

> *It will be after times of disasters and of great misfortunes, when harried peoples begin to breathe. Then imaginations, shaken by terrible*

spectacles, will depict things unknown by those who did not witness them.

Genius is timeless: but the men who carry it within themselves remain benumbed unless extraordinary events heat up the mass and make them appear. Then feelings pile up in the breast, torment it; and those who have a voice, anxious to speak, release it and relieve their minds.

That second condition has been fully met to permit our literature to be born. As a matter of fact, the essential part of the interest aroused by Black literature is due to the sum of experiences lived by Black people, in Africa as well as in America, individually and collectively.

To plagiarize Diderot: the disasters and the misfortunes of colonization have given birth to Black literature.

What are the various aspects of that literature?

Black literature was born in anguish, in a period of sorrow. The first characteristic of our literature is *outrage!*

Black literature is first of all a literature of combat. The writer throws himself into demands for retribution: the rights Black people have been deprived of by foreign domination must be recovered; Black people's place among the other peoples of the world must be demanded.

Let us cite some examples:

Adalberto Ortiz: (Spaniard, Ecuador). The author of *Yujungo*, that hero whom domination had deprived of those dearest to him: his wife and his only child, and who kills to recover his liberty and avenge himself on his enemy.

Chief A. B. Luthuli: (South Africa). All his strength stretches out to liberate his people; one of his works is entitled *Liberty for my People*.

Jacques Roumain: (Haiti, born in 1907, died in 1945). He opposes American occupation with all the violence of his style; his eye is to the full restoration of his country's rights.

Persuasion: The literature of *persuasion* consists of songs about the misfortunes of the Black man, his despair, but also his hope, his belief in a better tomorrow.

Jacques Roumain: In his principal book, *Masters of the Dew*, the writer wants to convince the enemy, to bring him to understand, to incite him to pity over the fate of the people. He doesn't mince words, but he avoids hate and coarse methods. Banishing all sentimentality, he appeals to reason.

The image he presents to his people is of poverty and the death of the Black man.

"We shall all die," he states at the beginning of his novel.

That fact returns in the form of an echo, sober and lyrical:

"Yes, in truth, the Negro is a poor creature."

L. S. Senghor: His whole work is a canticle of love addressed to the soul and to reason. This is the essence of the sweetness of his poetry. Senghor aims above all at convincing, at persuading. Senghor is a negotiator.

"Songs of Darkness" are among his poems; in them hope and nostalgia divide the Black soul.

The Poetry of Négritude: All this literature, whether of combat or persuasion, whether it aims at tearing out by force the rights refused to the Black man, or at obtaining them by poetic and literary negotiation, is always a committed literature, a literature conceived for a cause—the cause of Black emancipation.

It is a literature of refusing all that is not true to the Black African self. It is the literature of *négritude.*

What does the term *négritude* mean? When was it born? What area does it cover? What are its limits?

Its origins: The term was launched by Léopold Senghor and two of his friends, Aimé Césaire and Léon Damas.

This term assumes, as we shall see, a true Black self-awareness, a self-awareness that began to stir America in about the 1920s.

It was in the Afro-Caribbean area that *négritude* was born. Passing through Fort-de-France (Martinique) and Port-au-Prince (Haiti), *négritude* took up residence in the Latin Quarter in Paris where Léopold Sédar Senghor, Aimé Césaire and Léon Damas gave form to it.

For them *négritude* quickly became a profession of faith in the destiny of Africa. And it was a progressive creed:

1. *Négritude* is a question first of all of becoming aware of the existence of Black values, of coming to know that all one's thoughts (and expressions) should be African.

2. *Négritude* is next a way of thinking and of writing about Black values.

3. *Négritude* is still more a liberation; it is a question in fact of renewing African tradition in contact with the modern world—it's being liberated.

4. Moreover, *négritude* transcends those rediscovered values in order to climb toward the universal, where the fusion of all civilizations is achieved; for in the conception of Senghor and of most men of Black African culture, there will be a universal civilization which will be in some way the amalgamation of all known civilizations; and Black civilization will play an essential role in creating that civilization.

5. The term *négritude*, finally, translates a conscience, the Black conscience. In fact, a double feeling divided the soul of the writers and of all Blacks, a feeling that this literature tries to express.

a) The Black man is a being who sees himself as having lost his "self," as being disintegrated by violence and the weight of the presence of an invading foreign element. The Black man is devoured by the fear of not being black enough. Numerous writers have expressed that fear in poetry, as we shall now hear.

The Ghanaian poet, Francis Ernest Kobina Parkes, confided that disquiet to us in his poem entitled *African Heaven:*

> *Give me black souls*
> *Let them be black*
> *Or chocolate brown*
> *Or make them*
> *The color of dust—*

Dustlike,
Browner than sand
But if you can
Please keep them black
Black . . .

The poet, and this is curious, seems to suggest that it is hard for him to remain black. Hence, that significant verse: "give me black souls."

Can we express any better the anguish of Blacks conscious of undergoing a metamorphosis?

b) But at the same time this black artist seems to be proposing to himself the idea that he was born after his time. That is an impression that the white power structure adds to by repeating to the Black from morning till night that he is lacking in maturity. That is why he has long been pushed aside from assuming responsibility for his own destiny.

And the Black asks himself what this backwardness is due to, since his race was probably born at the same time as the other races on our planet. Witness this melancholy exclamation of J. P. Kindamba:

"Man-eating Land"

Oh my country!
Last of inhabited lands
They say
And yet on the first day
At the same time as the others
You were created.

We can therefore define *négritude* as being a poetry of suffering, of moral and spiritual anguish which finds its source in physical and social anguish.

Limits of the term; its strength: Much fault has been found with the concept of *négritude*. Numerous works have proposed a thousand and one definitions which, instead of clarifying it, often dilute the concept and make it more obscure.

But the fact remains that for Africa the concept of *négritude* is an affirmation of Africa's presence and role in the concert of civilizations.

The West has often criticized that concept. First of all, it was said, the term was poorly chosen. But it is fitting firstly to ask oneself: poorly chosen to designate what? In order for a term to be declared poorly chosen, linguistically speaking, we must have clearly in mind the notions we want it to express. That is not the case here; it is a neologism by which we are trying to define disparate nuances whose whole forms the soul, the past, and the future of the Black world.

Phonetically speaking, it may sound unusual to the ear; but it is not more grating on the ear than words long accepted, such as *aptitude, attitude, longitude, latitude,* whose phonological composition is similar. A root—*niger* (black) + a suffix—*tude* (condition). Thus, *négritude:* condition of persons of the black race.

If its semantic content is complex and trouble-some, that, far from making the term detestable, ought only translate what has always existed, that is to say that the Black world had remained until then indecipherable, inaccessible; it will remain so as long as it is not defined in human terms: politico-economic and socio-cultural, as the West has been.

The term *négritude,* when put in this context, is no longer vague or imprecise. For it translates a state of being, a manner of belonging to a race.

It has also been said that the term *négritude* is restrictive and racist, and it has been said that it must open and enlarge its horizons so that those who are not Black may find in *négritude* a chance to live, to enrich themselves, and to deepen their own humanity.

That idea was advanced at the Conference on the Festival of Negro Arts in Dakar in April 1966.

We will say that *négritude* has never closed its doors. Although it is an affirmation of Black humanity, its goal is to meet all men and all civilizations at the summit; it is therefore in no way restrictive, in no way racist.

There are Blacks who have found in Western civilization an opportunity to enrich their own humanity; why would the West be refused a chance to enrich itself through contact with the rediscovered world of Black consciousness? All Westerners are welcome who unearth our past, so rich in its teachings, or who give life to our threatened dialects by codifying and stabilizing them.

Négritude and the African Personality: The international press has even tried to oppose *"négritude,"* the term used by French-speakers, and "African personality," the concept used by English-speaking Africans.

Négritude and African personality do not translate two different sociological systems, one applicable in the former English colonies, the other in the former French colonies.

Actually, if these two worlds have undergone different educations, their heart continues to be the same: they are Blacks who have long been scorned, long regarded as objects to be sold. For what gave birth to this concept expressed in two different ways is still the same, that is to say the desire of the Black world to meet squarely the humiliating situation imposed on it by the so-called civilized world.

From both sides, in fact, it has acted to defend and illustrate Black cultural values, to assert itself and thereby to make the Black continent and the Black world felt, and to survive.

Thus, there is no antinomy between the two expressions, but simply diversity in the translation of the same concept, of the same ideal.

Black Africans, writers and people, reject, therefore, on every level that absurd and fruitless quarrel over terminology.

Is Négritude Dated? Finally, it is said that the concept of *négritude* is old-fashioned and out of date, that it has, on the whole, seen better days and has now lost its bloom. That is disturbing, all the more so since one of the originators of the concept, Aimé

Césaire, publicly proclaimed from the podium of the Conference on the Festival of Negro Arts, at Dakar, in April 1966:

"I don't like the word *négritude* at all." Unfortunately, he does not say what he finds displeasing in the word. What he hastens to do is, on the contrary, to defend the term *négritude.*

"The expression *négritude*," he says, "has its qualities and its shortcomings; but it is disparaged and distorted; it must be defended by putting it back in the situation of Blacks at the moment when it was born, that is to say, between 1930 and 1940."

From the moment the concept of *négritude* was born, Césaire says, the Black man ceased to be vulnerable to attack by the White man.

Was this because the Black soul was inaccessible to White men? Unattainable? Did it reflect some inability to understand the realities of Black existence?

White men who have analyzed the Negro have never rehabilitated the authentic Black man. Instead, they have presented a caricature, an image distorted in the process by self-serving analyses; they have handed back nothing but a series of prejudices.

Authentic Blacks—poets, novelists, storytellers—had therefore no other recourse but to rise up against that humiliating situation.

Thus was born the literature of *négritude,* which is the rehabilitation of the Black man, and his restoration "in his original form." The expression is Césaire's. All that can be said in all frankness is that the literature of *négritude*, inasmuch as it is demanding, is now almost exhausted; for if it has produced a result—Black emancipation—it has also developed with the help of that movement.

Now, Africa's political independence is already almost a reality, with only a few exceptions. A literature conceived to make demands against foreign colonial powers will soon be out of date. It will still, however, have battles to fight for a long time to come. For with the independence of our countries, the Africans themselves henceforth have the responsibility to govern themselves and they sometimes tend to perpetuate the injustices of which the West had been guilty.*

The literature of *négritude* must, therefore, continue the fight; it can do this by rejuvenating itself through new themes, through a struggle against the people within its own household who have lost contact with the aspirations of the nation.

---

*For a detailed analysis, see Edward M. Corbett, *The French Presence in Black Africa* (Washington, D.C., Black Orpheus Press, 1972).

CHAPTER 3:
topics of inspiration

The topics which inspire Black literature are numerous. To start with, there are themes related to those already treated in the West.

love of nature
study of the native land
description of manners and customs

There are also more sorrowful inspirational themes which translate the cry of peoples long oppressed and alienated:

exaltation of négritude
expression of racial oppression
social demands

But all that is already to be found in Black writing.

For we are well aware of the disorder that reigns in the Black world.

First of all, the Black world remains a mystery. The few works written about it cannot describe it adequately. And the great Black poet, Langston Hughes, asserts: "Even if Africa's sky is furrowed by airplanes, its great jungle heart remains indecipherable."

Indeed, Africa is an almost-virgin world; we must explore it, discover it. But such discovery is made difficult because of the many forms of disorder already mentioned:

Psychological Disorder: Diverse and divergent tendencies tug at the African heart and the African jungle. This is reflected on the social level and brings about:

Social Disorder: The absence of a national conscience and of a sense of responsibility installs straw men in the seats of command against whom literature rises up with violence. Egotism aided by individualism causes the Black world to remain without very clear or positive social consciousness. This prevents unity and in turn creates:

Political Disorder: Society being very poorly organized, being governed by selfish laws often inspired by the simple desire for political domination by the elites of the Black world, is beset by confrontation and social agitation which results in division, the formation of multiple parties, and violence exercised by men in power. This violence even goes as far as to result in frequent political assassinations totally without justification.

Black African literature deplores this situation and seeks to humble every Black government which has such a conception of power. That is why Black writers separate into two classes all officials at whatever level they may be found:

Conscientious officials: They respect the person of the citizen and look out for his well-being, sometimes at the expense of their own person. When these conscientious men are mistaken, and they are told about it, they make amends, correct their errors, and if they are unable to make amends—human nature being limited—they wisely retire from power.

"Straw-men" officials: Certain writers such as Bloke Modisane of South Africa are particularly caustic about them. For the straw-man official, the big thing is power at any price. He is ready to sacrifice anything to stay in power. He suppresses all freedom, and uses violence to maintain his authority. The straw-man ridicules all who do not think as he does and who refuse to kiss his feet. He removes them from power by any means possible. This, evidently, favors:

Economic Disorder: The straw-man, entirely absorbed in strengthening his authority, does not have the time to form a viable, human, and healthy national economy. The state exists, therefore, on loans. The most important effort is sacrificed to the formation of large, well-trained, and burdensome forces of repression.

This is the kind of disorder which confronts the Black world today. Literature reflects this disorder, and it is therefore risky to try to find in literature a steady chronological development.

The Black world must first rediscover itself. And that rediscovery only begins at the moment when the Black world becomes aware of its own values, strengths, and weaknesses; when each person recognizes and demands his place in this great liberation movement, this rebirth of the Black man, or rather this rehabilitation of his most authentic values, heretofore unrecognized.

This rebirth is a vast movement: sudden, disordered, exalting, pathetic, dramatic, and tragic, all at the same time.

These are human miseries of which Racine could have made a tragedy, but a tragedy not on the scale of an individual, nor of a family, as he often did, but of a race, as Robert Garnier did in *The Jews*.

This rebirth is, to begin with, disordered, sudden, exalting, because the Black world is caught between two fronts: the foreigner and the Black himself who sells out to the White world.

Next, this renaissance is pathetic: the Black world has indeed been literally crushed by a weight that is very heavy, too heavy; the weight of colonization with its advantages, but, alas, with all its drawbacks also; the first of these was the deportation of Africans beyond the Atlantic, followed soon by the conquest of Africa, then its division to the benefit of the powers which certainly had no need of colonized slavery to survive.

This pathetic state brought about by the loss of our liberties is one of the most direct causes of the birth of Black literature.

This pathetic state assumes an astonishing breadth today; since even freed from the foreign yoke, the Black world still feels the weight of persecution imposed by those in power.

Obstacles, then, create our literature. Psychological and physical shock is the starting point of this literature, which is at first sorrowful and anguished, but quickly becomes militant.

Here as examples are two poems, one against foreign power, the other against Negroes who sold out their race.

"Between the Bible and the Whip"

The Bible in one hand
And in the other the whip,
This is the way from the start
That they presented themselves to my father.
But for that,
I will always forgive them
They are what we are.

Then surrounding themselves
With barbed-wire strands, they said:
"Leave this forest"
Thus they dispossessed
My father of his lands
But for that,
I will always forgive them
They are what we are.

Meanwhile a wild thought sprang up
In their minds: "Who will till the land?"

Thus they snatched
From my father's flesh
The fruit of his labors.

At cotton-raising time
They became masters
But at school, no place
Was found for them
Would not their exertions,
Oh, sorrow! support the "men"
Forever.
It is for that that I will never forgive them.

As long as I live.

                                    —*J. P. Kindamba*

"Go Back in Your Shell"

Returning from the woods, the other day
I met, on a bumpy road
A giant pearly snail
Who had, for his entire fortune,
Only his enormous shell
He stopped in front of the children.
Frightened by that mass
These defenseless innocents
Began to weep and cry
Then softly I drew near
That horrible thing

And said to it indignantly:
"Don't you know, giant snail
That you are frightening these children?
Go back to your nothingness
You dirty beast, and stay there
And, crestfallen, his eyes clouded,
He crawls back in his empty shell
They say he's still there.

—*J. P. Kindamba*

In the third place, this renaissance has become *dramatic:* in the sense that it began as a physical, spiritual, and moral struggle whose outcome was long uncertain for the Black world.

There is the struggle against assimilation. There is the struggle also to penetrate a milieu in which one is constantly rejected. That is one of the themes developed by Ferdinand Oyono in *Houseboy.*

That uncertainty often degenerated into resignation, into passive acceptance of outside domination or of the armed dictatorship of the Negro in power.

Finally, that rebirth has become tragic in the classic sense. One of the questions posed was: Was Africa created simply to be a servant? Is God the creator the same for the West as for the Negro world?

That question pulls a sorrowful answer from Jacques Roumain in *Masters of the Dew:* "No," he says, "God is white."

And since "God is white," the Negro shall himself be the artisan of his liberation, of his liberty— by rebellion, by work. That will be the new religion that Manuel inaugurates in Fonds-Rouge, in Haiti.

Such is the progress of the psychological movement which created the Black African literary movement and engendered at the same time the political struggles which shook the Black man to make him aware of his underlying nature and of his role in his milieu.

But the Black, not having been prepared for this fight, lived for years in that frightful psychological, political and economic disorder that we referred to earlier. As we have also noted, this disorder influences literature itself, for we are witnessing an abundant and disparate literary production. In it are found works with a message and works under Western influence, demanding a great "dewesternizing" effort in order to approach the edges of that still inaccessible African jungle.

A disparate literary movement, therefore, but one in which three phases can be distinguished.

There has been, first, a desire for the Black world to assert itself, to assert its existence, to exalt its soul, its Black soul, its freedom.

There has been, next, a real desire to become aware of its past, to make an earnest effort to inventory its cultural and artistic elements in order to rediscover a starting point for a strong and independent jump forward.

There has been, finally, the necessity of undertaking the urgent action required to assure a better future.

In order to assert himself, the Black writer wanted first to prove that the Black is not born a slave, that there is a native land with a glorious heritage to which he is linked by organic ties. And he owes it to himself to defend that land, to make it fruitful, to make it prosper. Unfortunately, wicked people came, and the sons of the Black country were deported beyond the Atlantic and others reduced to servitude on their own soil.

The theme of the native land provides a way to grasp the Black world, to understand the awakening of nationalism.

And because the description of the native land is linked to efforts to escape domination and to rediscover liberty and dignity, that description is in general devoid of serenity; it is rarely sensitive to the pure beauty of the landscape.

On the contrary, that description is formed of emotion, of memories, of nostalgia, or of anguish; the lyricism of those pages comes from protest against invasion.

Landscape painting is sometimes a cry of revolt against the misery imposed by rapacious natives who put themselves at the disposal of the imperialists.

But we note that this theme has been only slightly exploited and developed.

The general idea scattered through the texts of this type is a desire for permanence. In the preface of his collection of poems entitled *The Blue Soul*, Kindamba states: "As long as a drop of Negro blood still flows in our veins, we are Negroes."

And in a poem entitled "The Soil," he says in the last stanza:

Our forests and our savannas
Our mountains and our plains
And our waters are eternal.
We shall disappear as our fathers disappeared,
And the Soil remains. One day
The child must say: "My father passed this way."

The *soil* has here a double meaning: there is first
of all the land considered in relation to agriculture.
Beyond that it signifies the entirety of qualities and
shortcomings of the country in which one is born,
where one lives.

We feel, then, in the accents of this poem a very
high regard for the virtues of the common people, a
pride in the native land, to which we want to belong
with all our heart, and to which we return with joy to
plunge into its innermost recesses. Witness this Sierra
Leonean, Abioseh Nicol who returns from Cambridge
to his native soil singing:

"In the Depths of the Land"

And if I returned
Along Guinea's shores
Filled with intricate charms
Of our beautiful new cities
Dakar, Accra and Cotonou
Lagos, Bathurst, and Bissau
Then Freetown, or Libreville
Freedom is only in the mind.

They used to say: Go to the land
And see the real Africa

Wherever you come from
That's where you come from.
Go into the jungle—as far as you can
You'll find your hidden heart
Your ancestral soul,
Silent.

And I left
Dancing on my way.

The same accent is heard in a poem of Kindamba entitled "Native Land." Here the accent is
more melancholy, for the poet, happy to be back
home, sees himself feeling the gaze of his native land,
naked as Adam and Eve feeling the eyes of God on
them after their sin; to return to one's native land is
an enrichment; one comes back to clothe the heart.

"Native Land"

There is no more alluring land
Than one's native land.
One discovers it anew with heaven's charms

When, after a long absence,
One goes back there, all in rags;
One sees everything anew with a child's eyes,

Fresh in heart
Soul at peace
And flesh ready to receive
The caresses of a thousand dear hands;
Rock us, Oh native land:
Warm us, Oh blessed sun,

Wrap us in your misty veil
Oh protective Nature,
Here we are, impoverished and in rags;
Ready to inhale the nourishing breath

That your motherly soul sends us
Everything here breathes life:
The green hillside,
That supports my father's camel,
The deep vale to the South,
Rich with blue lakes
The northern slope watered by the Nzilla,
And the plain abloom with yellow gold
Everything here breathes peace
Hope,
Love.

Here we are impoverished and in rags,
Ready to throw ourselves again
In the ancestral ocean
To reinvigorate ourselves, prodigal children

And prepare ourselves for the big fight.

There is no more alluring land
Than one's native land,
One goes back there, all in rags
One sees everything anew, with a child's eyes,

Fresh in heart
Soul at peace
And flesh ready to receive
The caresses of a thousand dear hands
I found again with tenderness,
That peaceful place where mother rests.

I found again that giant palmtree
Pointing out to me again
The spot that witnessed my birth.
There used to be a hut there,
Built by my father,
To serve as my nursery.
The hut has disappeared,
And my umbilical cord also,
Both returned to the earth
To provide the giant palmtree
The sap that gives it life.
I found again that brook
That flows slowly
Where I stretched nets so fragile
That it took only the weak movement
Of an otter brook
To make them useless.
But there were no otters, and in the morning,

My nets were always quite full.
I found again that little grove
Become a forest of giants,
Where I used to stretch snares and traps

To catch the green pigeon
With so powerful a wing stroke,
Or the turtle-dove that flies so fast
I found all that again,
With tears in my eyes,
Fresh in heart,
Soul at peace,
And flesh ready to receive
The caresses of a thousand dear hands.

We are going to conclude the first part of this introduction to Black literature by saying that it is still in its beginning stage. But, although it has not yet produced writers as great as it is capable of producing, it has learned how to translate the aspirations of a soul that was for a long time the outcast of human society: I refer to the Black soul.

PART II:
a tragic tetralogy

*Under this heading we are going to analyze
quickly four Black African novels, four different
lives, four conceptions of a same single
reality: the tragic destiny of the Black race.*

They are:
Une Vie de Boy, *by Ferdinand Oyono,
translated as* Houseboy;
L'Enfant Noir, *by Camara Laye,
translated as* The Dark Child;
L'Aventure Ambigue, *by Cheikh Hamidou Kane,
translated as* The Ambiguous Adventure;
Gouverneurs de la Rosée, *by Jacques Roumain,
translated as* Masters of the Dew.

*These four novels form, in our view, a tetralogy
because, seen from a special vantage point, the
subjects of these works fall into a sequence.
The essential theme of these novels is the
leap, the penetration of the Black soul into
the Western world, a world foreign to its
customs.
That world has had three successive attitudes
toward the Black:*

1) Rejection
*Since the earliest encounters between the West
and the Black world, the West has had an attitude
of repulsion toward the latter. As a matter of
fact, the West thought that the Black world
was not capable of bearing the strains of*

Western civilization, of accommodating to it,
or of assimilating it. The Black man, it was
felt, was not worthy of Western culture and
thus had to be turned away from its closely
guarded inner stronghold.
That attitude is described by Oyono in
Houseboy. Toundi, the hero of the story,
is very curious—perhaps too curious. He wanted
to penetrate too quickly into the mysterious
European world by two routes: one religious,
with Fathers Gilbert and Vendermayer; the
other technical, with the White doctor, the
agronomist, and the administrator.
But he is forcefully rejected by each; and
by his death—which comes as a result of the
wounds the West inflicted on him—the West
refuses him the possibility of passing on to
the Black world the modest learning he was
able to acquire while he was in contact with
Western civilization.

2) Assimilation

But the West learned very early that it was
obliged to open out, whether it liked to or not,
to the Black world. From then on, the West
attempted to make the Blacks not producers,
but simple consumers of "civilization."
The Black man was assimilated as much as possible
in order to accomplish this. He was taught
the language of colonization and made to
believe that his own language was inadequate
for expressing human values. He was also led
to believe that his own society was

"barbarous" and "primitive," while Western life, in both its religious and technical dimensions, was presented as the best of all possible worlds.
This conception of assimilation is developed in Camara Laye's Dark Child. *The hero of the work, attracted by the Western mirage, becomes a prisoner of this sorcery. He will not return to Guinea. He represents that part of Africa—that easily influenced segment of the Black world—which forgets its heritage very quickly in order to continue to be accepted by the Western world.*

3) Liberalism
Nevertheless, the West has become, even for the Black world, a city built on a mountain; it is visible from every direction. Its light is capable of illuminating the Black world. Unfortunately, the Black man has not been able to use that abundance of light to see within himself and around about him. Instead of building itself up, the Black world quickly became fratricidal.
That is the condition of the world of the Black traced in Kane's Ambiguous Adventure *and in Roumain's* Masters of the Dew.

In The Ambiguous Adventure, *the Black world has leaped into the West to adapt itself to the sacred flame. But that light was extinguished at the very edge of the Black world,* by an impetuous tempest produced by the atmospheric pressures of the Black regions themselves.

In Masters of the Dew, the Black world, having made the leap into the West, has adapted to the sacred flame, has brought it back toward its own people to try to illuminate the primitive paths. The light will be kept, somehow or other. But the Black world becomes bogged down in internal struggles for mastery.

Manuel, assassinated by Gervilien, is of course, the symbol of the Black world in which people never stop fighting and killing each other, because they have not yet learned to place the interest of the community above that of the individual.

We shall indicate below the most striking aspects of this tragic tetralogy.

CHAPTER 4:
houseboy

discovery of a new world

A work apparently without depth and dealing with well-known themes, *Houseboy* is really a novel which opens up a new world not only for Toundi, its hero, but also for all Blacks.

A simple act begins to unlock this discovery: punishment.

The fact is that Toundi is punished for being too greedy after a religious gave him a piece of sugar. And having fled the paternal hearth, he lands in a world that he tries to know and to penetrate as the days go by. That world is composed of two sides—an outer side and an inner side.

The outer side: This side will teach him that the society of the Whites—which he first encounters in the fictional city of Dangan—is better organized than that of the Blacks. Dangan has a social hierarchy, a

59

hierarchy of values, division of labor, agreements for humane ends, social contracts to make the vicissitudes of life bearable.

He will also learn that to live happily in this world certain conditions will have to be met. In the first place he must have money. He will have to know how to read and write. He will have to have a profession, and he will have to more strictly apply the rules of hygiene.

In other ways Toundi becomes aware that there is a distance between the life of Whites and that of Blacks in Dangan. There is even a difference between the well-off Blacks of Dangan and the other Blacks.

There is only one thing for Toundi to do. He must try to meet at least a part of these conditions. He will succeed only imperfectly, but, because of his determination to do so, he moves quickly to perform all the domestic chores of Fathers Gilbert and Vendermayer, and then of the commandant of Dangan.

But Toundi is too attentive to the problems of the hour; his mind goes beyond the superficial world and penetrates the inner world.

The inner side: This is the moral and spiritual world. Very quickly Toundi becomes aware that although it is well organized, this world is only outwardly perfect. A series of revelations will open his eyes. What are they?

First revelation: He learns that the Black man cannot be happy in this artificial world built on racial segregation: there is no mixing between Whites and Blacks. This world is built on injustice and cruelty. Toundi is a ready-made victim for this injustice and this cruelty and he eventually dies because of it. This White world, he realizes, is built on scorn, which reduces the Black to the level of an animal; on prejudice, which makes the Black the eternal good-for-nothing; on social exploitation, which makes the Black a slave; and on corruption, which deadens the conscience.

But Toundi will very quickly understand also that the White acts like a wolf not only toward the Black, but also toward the White, and this will be the second revelation.

Second revelation: Toundi becomes aware that Whites are not as advanced on the moral and spiritual level as they are materially. In fact, he finds slander, treachery, disrespect, adultery, avarice, and greed to be commonplace in the White world.

Whites rip each other apart, and the Blacks pay for this misconduct. He changes when he comes in contact with this wicked and inhuman world. That will be the third revelation.

Third revelation: Toundi discovers that as a result of contact with the White experience, the Black heart is gnawed by the desire to exploit and deceive the White, by the desire for vengeance, and by scorn for the White. Toundi is more and more moved by sympathy for the oppressed, by racial solidarity, and eventually he decides on an open struggle against the oppressor.

Unfortunately, the Black has a well-known weakness: religion lulls him; and Fathers Gilbert and Vendermayer can make Toundi believe anything at all in the name of religion. There is no good argument against the White man's superiority. That is the fourth revelation.

Fourth revelation: Toundi learns at last that the Black, in this new world, is still an earthen pot competing with an iron pot; for he is powerless against the White world's brute strength, whose police, symbolized by Gosier-d'Oiseau, crush everyone.

Moreover, he is poor. Does not the houseboy's life symbolize the servitude to which the Black world has been reduced?

He is unfortunate: Toundi's escape is an unfortunate adventure.

He is inefficient: no responsibility is given the Black doctor, for he can take care of nothing. Unable to work things out, he is permitted to operate only on Blacks, never on Whites.

He is uncomplaining: when he is tortured, Toundi does not make a sound; that is a symbol of the resignation which relates Toundi to Vigny's wolf, which dies without a sound; for "to moan, weep, or pray are equally cowardly." That leads naturally to impassiveness; there is not, in fact, the least idea of revolt among the Blacks of Dangan; and the victim will die without defense. Why is that? Because there is not yet a real Black self-awareness.

The writer is therefore ahead of his hero. He is aware of it and does not seem to want to overexcite his characters before the hour set by fate, these minds not yet being properly prepared for rebellion.

We may conclude by saying that *Houseboy* without having the depth of the three other novels in the tetralogy, is without doubt one of the most eloquent indictments ever addressed by the Black world to the world of the exploiting colonizers.

The novel establishes also the failure of the Whites faced with the imperturbable attitude of the Blacks, the Whites having no strength but force.

In the final analysis, for Ferdinand Oyono, between Whites and Blacks there is no true lasting community: the Black remains a Black among Blacks, and the White remains completely distinct.

Ferdinand Oyono: Realist Writer: Realism is a movement of reaction to romantic art. The romanticists, breaking with the conventional art of the pseudo-classicists, professed to be writing works true to life. But they were loath to record the humdrum of daily existence, and they presented in their writing, not average people, but almost superhuman heros.

It was against this search for the grandiose that the realists reacted. Taking the opposite course, they describe simple, modest, obscure lives, lived in humble, even miserable surroundings.

Is not *Houseboy* the study of the life of average people? Is it not linked by the daily commonplaces it analyzes to the realist movement, even though it was conceived more than a century after the first realists? What are the arguments in favor of this thesis?

Observing reality: Ferdinand Oyono seeks first of all to unmask man, both black and white. And there is nothing which can reveal it better than:

His physique: each character has a particular behavior, unusual gestures: Gosier-d'Oiseau, the policeman; Kalesia, the loose woman; the agronomist;

Sophie, the commandant's wife; and especially the commandant himself, heavyset and burdened with thick calves.

His temperament: each individual is described with precision, from Toundi's father to the Greek, Janopoulos, and including the priests, Gilbert and Vendermayer, the catechumens, the Whites and the Blacks of Dangan.

As with the temperament, the comportment of individual people is often conditioned by their surroundings. Oyono paints the settings for his characters carefully.

Dangan is described vividly: the White quarter with its fine well-lighted houses; the black quarter, built on a dried-out swamp and immersed in darkness. The prison with its torture program. The hospital and its segregation. The market, where the commandant's wife is looked on as a princess. The church and the convent where the negress is subjected to the whim of the priests.

For Oyono, each of these settings is distinguished by a characteristic philosophy, and it becomes the psychology of the individual who lives there:

The Whites congregate and speak in malicious and slanderous terms of the Blacks.

Gosier-d'Oiseau becomes a cruel policeman, knowing that Blacks are under his control; the prison warden behaves in similar fashion.

The Blacks, for their part, cluster together and become envious and scornful at the slightest excuse, ready to make common cause and league together, passively of course, against the White oppression.

The houseboys' social class, spying on everything, discovering everything, makes fun of everything.

In sum, the contribution of the imagination is minimal in *Houseboy*; fiction is foreign to it. Here we are dealing only with an experience that really occurred and was transposed to the romantic level.

As it deals with lives in modest circumstances, *Houseboy* is:

The expression of everyday monotony: Oyono expresses simply what he sees and what he hears; he constantly lets his character speak without intervening. In that he is impersonal; for he does not judge, he is not obviously taking sides for the Whites or for the Blacks. How does he manage to do that?

By the form of the novel: It is in the form of a diary—thus of a document where the facts are noted without commentary, chronologically. That absence of commentary makes Oyono's style rather unpolished. What is noted are sometimes the most insignificant details of existence, or what should not be noted: a kick, the abuse inflicted on the women, Kalesia's unseemly utterances, or Madame's little bags that Toundi has to pick up, even from under her bed.

The absence of commentary maintains objectivity. Oyono describes the day-to-day existence by expressing commonplace things in detail.

By presentation by details: That search for the stimulating detail is successful because Oyono is endowed, not with the gift of imagination, but with the faculty of observing, of penetrating souls. Behavior is sometimes present by suggestion:

Gosier-d'Oiseau and the bananas: significant details to express the attitude of the White policeman toward Blacks.

Kalesia: big buttocks; a single earring; a jacket over her *pagne* that conveys a condition of extreme poverty.

These details are scattered through life and, using the diary form, the author finds them everywhere: the sugar that attracts the children and destroys them; Madame's sanitary napkins, the little bags; the kisses of Madame and the prison warden; Kalesia, who will greet Mr. Watercloset, to whom one never raises one's hat, but one's *pagne*; the minute descriptions of these miserable hovels; the hospital orderly who drinks alcohol in place of the wine he doesn't have. And it is the combination of details that makes *Houseboy* a work of art, and which gives us a complete image of that little place called Dangan. For life is "an accumulation of little circumstances."

As a matter of fact, isn't Toundi's life a sequence of little circumstances? But more than an observer, Oyono is a moralist, for he draws a moral from all these observations.

The Moral: A lesson should always emerge from a work of art; an indirect lesson. Of course, the artist will rarely depict good; for good is only an accident in man's daily life, and evil the normal behavior.

Is *Houseboy* something other than a portrayal of evil? That evil incarnated by all Dangan's Whites—the White doctor, Father Vendermayer, the commandant and his wife, Gosier-d'Oiseau—and likewise in all the Blacks.

That portrayal of evil, fortunately, is corrected by the presence, more or less visible, of virtue: the scorned and humiliated Blacks bear this condition without the least desire for revenge. Toundi endures the big foot of the commandant, who crushes his fingers. The African doctor endures the humiliation of his White colleague; he is not even worthy to keep the keys of the radio; and he is permitted to operate only on Blacks since in the White doctor's view they are almost animals, and therefore of no value. Toundi dies an innocent man, a victim of violence, of the White world's cruelty. But his death is a liberation; for his diary, in which he had recorded the observations made by his soul, can at last be turned over to both the oppressed and their oppressors.

We are going to conclude by asking ourselves if Oyono's realism is complete and total.

Toundi's death translates the great disappointment of the Black world. And this world thus may conclude that there is no salvation for it.

In another way Oyono is involved in the struggle, for Toundi is oppressed Africa; he is, finally, Oyono himself, even if our writer had never worked as a houseboy. The writer Oyono-Toundi cannot, therefore, totally rid himself of his original subjectivity. And we may borrow this thought of Flaubert who felt the writer should avoid allowing himself to be caught up in the social mechanism, for, "we see poorly what we are deeply involved in."

Thus, *Houseboy* is too committed a work to be impartial and wholly objective.

CHAPTER 5:
dark child
theme
of the child

Most novels or literary works deal with people of social and moral maturity. When the author must find words to put in the mouths of mature people with some experience of life, the task is relatively easy.

In *The Dark Child*, Camara Laye has a child do the talking—a child, the beginning of the man and the father of the man. Here, the task is obviously harder. For he has to develop two people in one: the grownup, Camara Laye, whose task is to retrace his life; and a child, the child that Camara Laye was. How does he see himself? How does he see the child? He sees himself and the child under various aspects.

The child contrasted with grownups: In comparison with adults, the child is characterized by his confident attitude toward life, nature, and man. He is frank and unaffected; he believes everything and tries everything. That confidence is so strong that the most dangerous animals become simple playthings. Witness this child's game with the snake; and the child himself states: "I went up close... I laughed, I wasn't afraid."

The child is entirely opposite to the adult. The latter, indeed, is suspicious, afraid of everything, although nurtured by experience. This is shown by Danany, the little apprentice. And by Camara Laye's mother who cruelly crushes the snake that had wandered into the compound.

The child is thus confident in the present as he lives it, and little concerned with the future that he still does not know. Neither does he glance backward to a past he did not know.

But experience has made the adult a tyrant: experience led her to fear the future, and she broke into the child's conscience like a housebreaker and pulled out of him promises that he made against his will—the child who had just been playing with the snake. He is spanked and promises not to do it again: "I promised," he said later, "although the danger in my play was not clear to me."

Where feelings are concerned, the adult is unconstrained. Thus, Aunt Awa, in Conakry, wanted to know what was taking place in Marie's heart in the presence of the Camara child—base curiosity.

But the child reacts instinctively; he senses an attempt to penetrate the secret recesses of his heart. He answers Aunt Awa by asking questions, intending to put her on the wrong scent.

The child thus conceived, this child who had never known the past, who looks at the present through a transparent mirror, and who is ignorant of the future, must learn everything and open out to the world by accumulating for himself the sum of knowledge needed to become an adult.

The child discovering the world: The first aspect of this world that the child learns to approach is the family hut. In the hut the child penetrates the secret of the family. Thus he will learn that the family's protection is assured by the *gris-gris,* the family guardian spirit, and especially by the totem, which is the most eloquent testimony of the omnipotence of the child's mother.

Next the child becomes aware that he belongs to a given family, to which he will succeed. Thus, a key theme of the novel is the importance of heritage.

But especially the child learns the great law of nature: work. First, work in the fields: the earth must be made to produce what is needed for the life of the family. It is, in sum, a matter of cultivating and keeping up this garden that God entrusted long ago to the first humans of the earth. The work of the land has rites that must be known, in which one must be initiated.

Working with gold requires purification and obedience to certain demands.

The child can learn to know this foreign world only through initiation.

The initiation period is taken up entirely with rites and prohibitions; one must be initiated to material things and to secret things.

Initiation to Material Things

By positive methods: children must learn certain rules, for example: take off wet clothes to avoid falling ill; wash one's hands before eating. At the same time, children will learn good manners; they will be required, for example, to say "thank you" to their mother after each meal.

By negative methods: here we consider all the prohibitions that complicate the child's initiation period: he is forbidden to look at older people during meals, to chatter during meals, to pick the choice piece of meat, etc.

Initiation into Secret Life

At the smithy: the secrets of the smithy are not divulged indiscriminately; work in gold, in particular, is the prerogative of the head smith; he is the one the little black snake visits; it is the prerogative, therefore, of the man who knows how to purify himself, who can abstain from all relations with women, for gold is purity itself, and only those pure in body and soul should touch it.

In the fields: there are numerous rites to complete: before the harvest, the beat of the drum should announce the beginning; the first swath is cut. During the harvest, certain rites must also be observed: no whistling, no picking up dead wood, for, says Camara Laye, "These are things which immediately bring bad luck."

Life beyond the grave: that is a mysterious life; the dead must never be invoked aloud.

theme of the child   73

Initiation by Trial

The first ordeal: fear. Children must, of course,
learn to overcome fear. This is an important stage to
get over in order to pass into adulthood. The elements of this ordeal are night, darkness, and roaring
lions.

The second ordeal: circumcision. The child is an
incomplete, an imperfect being; he will not be complete until he has been circumcised; he will then be a
grown man. Now this ordeal is at the same time the
ordeal of physical pain; the child must learn to bear
pain without the slightest outside sign.

The third ordeal: love. This is perhaps the hard-
est. Indeed, to this point all the ordeals were collective, even circumcision. This time the child will struggle alone, for the ordeal is individual. The ordeal is all
the more difficult because the child is already a man;
hasn't he been circumcised? Love, it seems to him is
now permissible, all the more so since he is beloved of
Marie. Moreover, Aunt Awa encourages him in that
direction.

But there again the child will emerge victorious,
for hearts, he decides, are isolated islands that can be
reached not with canoes nor with words, but with
thought. And then, to the argument of the sacred (for
love is sacred), the child adds the argument of age,
which he has not yet attained. And this is the final
victory which finishes making the Camara child a mature man, initiated into the life of his ancestors.

The fourth ordeal: the attraction of the outside
world. Camara lives at a moment which is a turning

point of history. And it is the attraction of the outside world which is going to sow trouble in this soul which until then has overcome all obstacles. The outside world is going to upset the Camara family, united until this moment, and arm its members against each other. The desire to escape is a very cruel temptation, and the child will give in to it. For the call of the West is so powerful, so irresistible, that the child risks losing his heritage to answer it. The family spirit cannot be transmitted to him, for to receive that he would have to continue to be his father's heir and continue to be attached to the soil.

The child is so befuddled he no longer knows what he should do: "I no longer knew whether I should continue to go to school or stay in the workshop."

Perplexed, he asks, "Father, what is the best thing for me to do?"

No one can answer that anguishing question, neither the father nor the mother, nor the other members of the family. Therefore a compromise is necessary: the child will go away, but on the condition that he come back, that he not be permanently captured by the West. The parents give way. The child, for his part, promises to succeed and to return.

Analyzing *The Dark Child*, we note that the author presents a precocious child, who asks questions worthy of a mature man.

But by that candor, by his simplicity, and especially by his wish to escape, *The Dark Child* promises other, and perhaps still more moving moments.

A departure always leads to thoughts of a return. The departure of the Camara child for France opens the novel, which stays open; this signifies that we await the return of the child to his native Upper Guinea, to fulfill the promise made to his father. The Black child must return as does Samba Diallo, the hero of *The Ambiguous Adventure*. Because when it is open the novel creates uneasiness; closed, it brings an answer, composure.

CHAPTER 6:
ambiguous adventure
africa
at the crossroads

The attempted assimilation of Africa into Western civilization was not accepted willingly. From the beginning, intelligent and alert Africans understood that they were being tempted to renounce their heritage. Witness the opposition of the traditional chiefs to the explorers. Thus it was only after a long struggle that the West, superior to Africa in arms and in other material ways, succeeded in conquering the Black continent.

The acceptance of the West by Africa was not a voluntary choice, but a defeat. And no one could imagine what the consequences would be.

The Struggle

The struggle against the Western invasion was dictated by three tendencies:

The will to remain Black Africans: This is the first sign of the struggle against the invader. All Black African writers of note affirm the value of Blackness, struggle to maintain the Black world's values, and reject once and for all any tendency toward a metamorphosis of the authentic lifestyle of the Black world.

In a word, the matter before us is the assertion of Black personality, past, present, and future. And to assert that personality, Samba Diallo—the central character of Cheikh Hamidou Kane's *The Ambiguous Adventure*—must refuse to go to the foreign school, for the Diallo family senses vaguely that the foreign school threatens to transform them by injecting in their children the germ of a new way of life.

The family feels that the foreign school is a lotus whose fruit made the foreigners forget their native land; it is, therefore, a dangerous fruit. But soon anguish springs up, for a question is posed, and it is Samba Diallo—who Kane paints as the interpreter of African anguish—who poses it: "But do we still have enough strength to resist the school and enough substance to remain ourselves?"

The will to satisfy Black African needs: African needs are numerous; they assail us on all sides says Samba Diallo. And faced with them, the desire to remain oneself is only an illusion: "We are already conquered by the answers, apparently infallible, that the school gives to these needs. This means that we are played out, our substance is exhausted."

Our material substance: we must improve our economic system under the influence of Western methods.

Our moral substance: do we still have enough will to resist the enemy?

Our spiritual substance: our religions are threatened by the Christian religion. Is it worth more than all our religions put together?

These are some of the questions that Cheikh Hamidou Kane poses. They are disturbing because they apparently prove that Africa, turned toward the foreign school, that bewitching mirage, is already irreversibly sliding in the direction of the West.

The will to resist the foreign school and complete change: The Diallobes are irreversibly attracted by the foreign school of which they know nothing. Only the Chief Teacher penetrates the mystery and puts to the schoolteacher the following question: "What good news do you teach, therefore, to the children of men, to make them desert our centers of learning in favor of your schools?" But the schoolteacher's answer is vague: "I put my child in the school because I had no choice." Thus, it is impossible to do otherwise; the foreign school irresistibly attracts the whole of Africa. And it is the very uncertainty about the nature of the school—a mirage, that becomes an object of curiosity—which takes the African captive. And this weakens his resistence and hastens his fall and ultimate defeat.

Defeat

There are three steps in the African's defeat:

Weakened Africa: Africa is weakened because it is divided. The Diallobes have the same ideal: they "want to learn how to fasten pieces of wood together better," that is, to build a solid hut. But they don't agree on the way to do it. Thus two voices speak for Africa.

The voice of the Chief Teacher: The Chief Teacher symbolizes conservative Africa, living in nostalgia for the past. He wants Samba Diallo to be taught according to custom, because he must remain himself, without mixture, without physical, cultural, or spiritual crossbreeding. Samba Diallo must remain a gourd whose vocation is "to stick lovingly to the soil." Because if the gourd misses its vocation, if it feels the need to fly away, it will become empty and full of echoes.

Unfortunately, the gourd has already taken off on its flight, for Samba Diallo is already wearing new clothes which symbolize a great change. The Chief Teacher tears them off him, so that Samba Diallo may reclothe his heart by immersing himself again in the life of the Diallobes.

To the Chief Teacher these new clothes are only a lure, a decoration, an exterior varnish which does not clothe the heart. Thus the African explanation of the foreign school is for the Chief Teacher synonymous with ungluing, uprooting, and going astray. But his efforts are hopeless because the voice of the West is more insistent than ever.

The voice of the High Princess: The High Princess represents that Africa already open to new impressions, that Africa which no longer hesitates, and which accepts new clothes for its children. She accepts the foreign school and its innovations. The future of Africa is at stake.

Thus Africa finds itself at a crossroads. It would stay there if a compromise did not appear.

Compromise

Africa had to avoid choosing the wrong road, and compromise is the only means of salvation for Africa. Each way mentioned above has its advantages and its drawbacks.

The African way (the one chosen by the Chief Teacher): if the Diallobes are not in school, they will remain themselves. But they are threatened, because their huts will fall in ruins and their children will die or be reduced to slavery.

The Western way (that of the High Princess): if the Diallobe children go to the foreign school, they will forget themselves; they will forget their own nature. But the loss will be compensated, Samba Diallo's father thinks; as a matter of fact, they will learn all the ways to fasten pieces of wood together "that we don't know." A compromise is therefore necessary.

The Diallobes will follow the two ways: this is really a compromise, and it will be the work of the young Chief Teacher, Demba, who becomes the new spiritual leader of the Diallobes after the first Chief Teacher dies. Demba is open to new ideas; he orders the children to go first to the traditional school and then to the foreign school in their leisure hours. In them two civilizations will be born and will develop at the same time.

This compromise is beneficent: The High Princess justifies her choice: doesn't the foreigner know "the art of winning without being in the right?" What an advantage, to be able to conquer the foreigner, the West, by using its own art. "The struggle has not ended yet" although the Diallobe ancestor has been defeated. That ancestor is the African spirit, the African soul.

The foreign school is a form of warfare, a new form not yet widespread. Those who know that form of warfare are an elite. Profit must be gained from the offer by sending the African elite to school for an education.

Samba Diallo will, therefore, go to school. It is at that moment that the big adventure takes form with still more precision. For the prophet had in some way permitted it when he said: "You will go to look for knowledge, if need be, as far as China."

Samba Diallo senses his destiny in a confused fashion. But he wants the dead to be consulted first; hence, he visits the old woman Rella in the cemetery who approves the decision. Nevertheless, despite the approval issued by the dead, this adventure remains uncertain and therefore "ambiguous."

Acceptance of the new school corresponds to passage to another life, and this disturbs the Diallobes: won't the foreign school, this kind of Lotus, rob the children even of the memory of their fathers?

Consequences

This choice that circumstances have rendered obligatory is full of grave consequences which justify the Diallobes' fear, because there is a *metamorphosis of Africa:* the West shapes Africa as fire shapes metal. And Samba Diallo's father finds the image for it. For him Western civilization is like a brazier in the center of which were roasting "dishes of human beings, all colors of beings, who, as they came closer to the flames, took on imperceptibly the surrounding pattern, and under the effect of the light, lost their original color to become the same blond tint that covered everyone around them."

The foreign school is a new birth: the Diallobes must die in the flames to be reborn, just as the field must be drained to produce, or the seed buried to give new life.

In his vision, Samba's father notes that the dishes of humans roasted in the fire lost their original color; they became pale. That is truly the metamorphosis, and Samba Diallo, full of anguish, expresses it in the following way:

> *It suddenly appears to us that all along our journey we have not stopped undergoing a metamorphosis and now we have become other than ourselves. Sometimes the metamorphosis isn't even finished; it leaves us in a hybrid stage. Then, filled with shame, we hid ourselves.*

And it is then that the question of the return to the fold is posed. Samba Diallo, having become a cultural halfbreed, no longer knows the way back. He has made, as it were, a leap into another world; he has forgotten everything, even how to pray.

At the present time Africa no longer hesitates. It no longer asks itself if it should go to the foreign school; it simply goes. But there are now many foreign schools, and the problem is to choose among them. Africa is attracted sometimes to the West, sometimes to the East.

In this ambiguous adventure, Africa is at a crossroads. By deciding on a compromise, Africa does not avoid the metamorphosis, which is a necessary evil.

Thus, we conclude that Africa must submit to compromise and metamorphosis, if it does not want to stay forever at the crossroads.

CHAPTER 7:
masters of the dew
god and the gods

One of the reasons the slavers offered when they were taking Blacks from Africa across the Atlantic was that they wanted to make Christians of them. Africans were not, it was argued, acquainted with the living God that was worshiped in Europe and the New World.

But the African slaves had gods of different origins. And on the religious level, a blending was inevitable, in the land of exile, between the Christian God, God of heaven, and the pagan gods, gods of earth. Jacques Roumain's *Masters of the Dew* offers an accurate and fascinating account of how this blending occurred.

There is in this novel an absence of living faith and a continual back-and-forth movement between the Christian God and the pagan gods. But the hero

of the novel, Manuel, raises up against this double
religion a new religion, active and efficacious: *sacred
work,* the same religion that the God of heaven instituted in the Garden of Eden in Chapter 2, verse 15 of
Genesis. And all this is seen by Jacques Roumain
under the angle of misery. The consciousness of misery, of the death which threatens the little society of
Fonds-Rouge creates a terrifying doubt in the soul of
its residents. They doubt the complete goodness, the
omnipotence of the God of heaven. They also doubt
the strength of the pagan gods, and they ask themselves who is responsible for the extreme poverty of
Fonds-Rouge. Thus arises the important question that
Jacques Roumain and Manuel try desperately to
answer:

Is God good? On first impulse the eyes of the
Black man in Haiti turn toward the God of heaven.
But disappointment is not slow to implant itself in
their minds, for God remains deaf to the anguished
cries of the wretched.

Is it because he is wicked or because he can do
nothing for downtrodden man?

Bien-Aimé is convinced of God's malice: isn't he
the creator of the world, of all in it, misery and evil?
God therefore willed misery and evil on Negroes.

But the Haitians of *Masters of the Dew* are convinced of God's imperfections; to them God, indeed,
is not perfect, as the Christian religion preaches all
day long. The people of Fonds-Rouge are convinced
that:

a) God cannot hear every prayer, which proves
the failure of his omnipresence.

b) He cannot answer every prayer, which means the failure of his omnipresence and of his omniscience.

c) He doesn't want to listen to the groans of the wretched; "he blocks his ears," and this is proof that his goodness is lacking.

All the residents of Fonds-Rouge are convinced not only that God is imperfect, but that he is not good. This is the conviction of Annaise, Manuel's fiancee, who does not understand how God, who is said to be so good, could permit Manuel's assassination at the moment he was about to erase poverty in Fonds-Rouge. It is also the conviction of Simidor Antoine who does not understand how God, who is said to be so good, could have instituted differences between Whites and Blacks.

That conviction is so strong among them, that they go so far as to conceive of the God of heaven as being racially white. "God is *good,* they say. God is *White* is what they should say."

The wickedness of God is concretized by his church on earth; that church whose stinginess is known to all, and which knows neither pity nor love.

The absence of love was proven when for lack of money, the body of the assassinated Manuel could not be taken to the church. The church sells its prayers. And the longest prayers and the best, those which sound genuine, which send the soul from hell to paradise, are said for those who pay the most.

The church sells salvation although paradoxically it never stops preaching that humble and obedient souls get the grace of God for nothing.

Thus the Negro in Haiti has not made the acquaintance of the living and good God. Therefore the pagan gods return.

Are the pagan gods helpful? Tribulation and misery have not made the Negroes of Haiti forget their past; they did not forget their African gods or their beliefs. Except Manuel. He was the victim of a second deportation; he spent fifteen years abroad.

Bien-Aimé reminds him of this openly when they drink to celebrate Manuel's return: "Bien-Aimé drank in turn, after spilling a few drops on the ground. 'You forgot the custom,' he grumbled. 'You have no respect for the dead; they are thirsty, too.'"

But since the Haitians can forget neither God nor the pagan gods, the result is inevitably a mingling of the two—both in external manifestations (the image of Saint James represents at the same time Ogoun, the Dahomean god) and in belief and prayer. But this mingling does not keep them from having great confidence in their pagan gods. They give thanks to the pagan gods, to *Papa Legba.* Isn't he the master of the crossroads who opened the road back for Manuel?

Yet the Negroes of Haiti very quickly became aware that these African gods were ineffective. The African *loas* are really not able to make rain fall: "We pray for rain, we pray for the harvest, we make our petitions to the saints and to the *loas*," but in vain.

Even sacrificing animals to these gods did no good. Thereupon the puzzled Haitian Negro asks himself: Is this misery the concern of God, of the gods, or of men?

Who is really responsible for Haiti's misery?
Jacques Roumain would like to show us that the
Haitians know God only superficially, through a few
attributes which show him to be an all-powerful being. In their eyes, "He is the Lord of all things; he
holds in his hands the changing of the seasons, he
holds the strings that control the rain and the life of
all created things. He is the one who gives light to the
sun and who lights the candles of the stars; he blows
on the day and it grows very dark."

This belief requires God to do everything—to
make it rain, etc.—while the people stand with folded
arms, demanding miracles. When God seems to give
nothing at all, when no miracles happen, they blame
all that goes wrong on him; he becomes for them a
bad and helpless god. If God, then, can do nothing
further for them, what can they do, poor creatures
that they are? Inevitably they give in to *resignation.*

Against this defeatist attitude, Manuel set up the
work-god, which is the opposite of resignation.

First of all, fields of action must be separated,
said Manuel: "There are things that concern heaven,
and there are things that concern earth."

This means that man himself should make use of
the strength and the intelligence with which God has
endowed him to deal with the things of earth, because "God has no business with these things."

Jacques Roumain does not believe in miracles.
Work is the greatest miracle that man should expect
from himself, for, as Victor Hugo said, if man has
come from the word of God, society will come from
the word of man through work.

Battle must therefore be joined with the land; it must be kneaded to make of it the salutary dough from which bread will come. That is providence, and no other should be expected. People must not, therefore, resign themselves to whatever may happen to them. Misfortune must not be accepted passively. Prayer must be unceasing, and the form of that prayer is *work*.

The conclusion that Manuel draws is that "it is not God who abandons the Negro; the Negro abandons the land, and he is punished for it by drought, poverty, and sorrow."

Haitian religious life is a mixture: the God of heaven with the gods of earth.

But already the god of modern societies is making its way with Manuel into this almost primitive community: the *work-god* which in certain cases causes the true God to be lost from sight, but which does not necessarily make people atheists.

The Water Theme

The water problem is the essential theme of the novel. For the whole thing is centered on the drought which struck Fonds-Rouge. It brings life to a halt in Fonds-Rouge, undermines faith in God, and haunts every mind with the thought of death. Manuel says, "This water question means life or death."

Are the Fonds-Rouge residents going to give up and let themselves die? Are they going to fight against this slow death to attain a full and healthy life, and to find again the material and spiritual waters they have lost?

Lost material water: Lack of water is synonymous with the desert. It is the cause of all temptation. It brings on hunger, thirst, and hate. It can lead to death, just as Délira-Délivrance foretells: "We are all going to die."

Lost spiritual water: When suffering and need dry up the soul and weaken it, the result is a spiritual desert. A heart without love is as dry as land without water. A dry heart is full of hate; it is this very hate that tears Fonds-Rouge apart when spiritual water is lacking. And if the heart dries out still more, the community dies. That is what happens in Fonds-Rouge, where the spirit of revenge, of slander, and of calumny sends out deep roots.

Both material and spiritual land must therefore be moistened; Fonds-Rouge must be given back the water it vitally needs. The hate that is tearing Fonds-Rouge apart will not disappear until the spiritual water, *love,* is found again, and that life-giving water will be brought back by reconciliation. For water washes and purifies; water renews and makes hearts serene again. And Manuel will bring the water of love back to Fonds-Rouge by reconciliation, by his death.

Water refound: To find spiritual water again through pardon and love is to find grace again through reconciliation.

When it is understood in Fonds-Rouge that hate does not build, that it is better to forgive Manuel's assassin (Manuel had not even wanted to reveal his name before he died) than to punish him, that Haiti's real enemy is poverty, and that poverty can be overcome only by united action, only then does the great *coumbite* foretold by Manuel come about.

The lack of water in Fonds-Rouge and its rediscovery are symbolic of the absence and the rediscovery of love. And the symbol is self-explanatory: the Negro world will build itself up only through unity and through love. Human misery, a misfortune which all share, and which reaches disquieting proportions in Negro societies, must be fought. To be overcome, this general misfortune must be attacked by all working together; and victory is impossible if the hearts of the fighting men are divided.

PART III:
death of the hero

In moving toward a more profound analysis of
Black African literature, I hesitated between
two possible subjects:

1. The theme of resistance.
2. The death of the hero in the novel.
To deal adequately with
the first of these subjects would lead us
straight to the rostrum of the United Nations
to strike the imperialist army with all the
strength nourished by the bitterness that so
many years of colonization have built up in
our aggrieved hearts.
We know that that would
have delighted our fellow citizens. But beyond
that what good would we have served? And our
action would seem moreover to reflect upon the
honor of the United Nations.
We have preferred, trying
to repeat as little as possible things already
known, to confront today's man with himself,
and to make him aware of the state of his
existence a few decades ago. That's why we
decided on the second subject.
We will not retell
here the history of Black literature; nor will
we follow a chronology or a classification of
Black literary works.
For, as we saw in
Part III, the Black world is still a world in
disorder—psychological, social, political, and
economic disorder. And literature feels the
effects of this disorder. It is therefore too

early to try to order this literature too systematically. The Black world must first rediscover itself. And that rediscovery will begin only at the moment when the Black world becomes aware of its existence in that great liberation movement which gives a rebirth and a rehabilitation to Africa's most authentic values.

This rebirth, we have argued, is a vast movement—sudden, untidy, exalting, pathetic, dramatic, and tragic—all at the same time.

Pathetic, *we said a moment ago, for Africa was literally crushed under the very heavy weight of colonization. And this pathos resulting from the loss of our liberty is one of the most direct causes of the birth of Black African literature. It is, therefore, the obstacle which created that literature. It is the psychological and physical shock which is the starting point of that sad, anguished literature, which quickly became a fighting literature. This movement follows the history of all literature—which is born generally of a shock or in reaction to a preceding movement.*

The movement became dramatic *at a very early stage because it initiated a moral and physical struggle the outcome of which was uncertain for Africa.*

That uncertainty often degenerated into resignation, into passive acceptance of outside domination. And it is

here that tragedy in the classic sense of the
term appears.
Was Africa conceived by
the supreme being simply to serve? Is this God
the creator in the same relationship with the
Black world as with the West?
That question forced a sorrowful answer
from Jacques Roumain: "No!" he answered:

"God is White."
And since "God is White,"
the African will be the creator of his own
liberty, through rebellion.
There, in broad terms,
is the progression of the psychology underlying
the Black African literary movement which, at
the same time that the political struggle began,
shook the Black man to make him aware of his deep
inner nature, and of his role in his surroundings.
But the African, not prepared
for this conflict, lived for decades in
frightening psychological disorder. This shows
up in the literature itself, the variety of which
made a deep impression on the great poet Langston
Hughes. Included in it are:

—Folk songs,
sung to the rhythm of the traditional tomtom,
and continually renewed.
—Folk tales
and legends passed on by word of mouth by
the minstrels.

—Novels and
short stories translating the deepest and
truest aspirations of the African.
—Deeply committed
social poetry.
—Works influenced
by the West or requiring "de-westernization"
in order to approach the edge of the still
inaccessible jungle.
In this varied literary movement
three phases can be found:
First, a desire
for Africa to assert itself, to assert its
existence, to exalt its soul, its African soul,
its freedom; to affirm its personality.
Second, a real desire
to learn about the African past, an earnest
effort to inventory its cultural and artistic
elements in order to find the basis for a
strong and independent movement forward.
Finally, a need to
undertake the urgent action required to assure
that past and thus to present a better future.

CHAPTER 8:
heros and their role

We have just summed up in three sentences the literary expression of the fight for the emancipation of the Black man. We will now turn our attention chiefly to the third phase, while drawing also on the other two, and ask ourselves what is the place of the hero in the Black African novel.

In some cases the Black African hero is the violent fighter ready to spit in the face of the colonizer, or to jump upon the ranks of the enemy, cutlass in hand, and to swing in every direction.

We have here a sample of that *literature of conflict* in which the hero is identical with the author; he throws himself into action to claim his rights, and because he is hungry, demands with his cutlass his place in the center of the banquet.

Such is first of all, Adalberto Ortiz; also Luthuli who shouts at the top of his voice: "Liberty for my people, or take the consequences." And to mention another, Jacques Roumain, the Haitian who threatens the invader in these prophetic words: "Try to be big shots, you bastards; some day you'll get a kick in the ass from our big farmers' boots."

Let us say immediately that in such a case, the hero perishes, riddled by the shells of the enemy, who is always skilled in the art of "winning, without being in the right," to use the words of one of the main characters in *Ambiguous Adventure*.

But often the hero is calm, acting less through violence than through gentleness. This is the literature of persuasion. And we put in the first rank the living hero, one of those who hammer out Black thought, Léopold Sédar Senghor, the poet of bewitching rhythms, who persuades by the gentleness of his poetry, and whom we cannot fail to mention, although we are dealing only with novelists.

Senghor blends his hero with himself, being himself the hero of his work; he prepares, in his work as in his life, the African future through persuasion.

The same applies to Samba Diallo, the hero of gentle Cheikh Hamidou Kane, and to Jacques Roumain, mentioned earlier, who, although violent in style, offers us a Black hero who is firm, but gentle and loving.

There are in Black African literature in general, and in the novel in particular, several kinds of heros:

1. The violent hero, fighting with cutlass or with bitter words.

2. The hero convinced of the importance of the struggle, and who bends to convince others through persuasion and dialogue.

3. The faint-hearted hero, who states a problem, but offers no solution, or who shirks his responsibilities as a Black man.

Our intention is to study the place, the role, and the fate of each of these heros: why some of them die, and what their death means. The violent hero is presented to us in the first phase of the struggle of the Black for his emancipation. The persuasive hero and the faint-hearted hero are presented to us especially in the third phase, the one which, drawing on the past and the present, prepares tomorrow's Black society.

Here, then, is posed the problem of the Black taking root in his society, in his milieu. Here the Black African hero will be confronted, but not with an outside obstacle (this phase has almost been passed by, on the literary plane at least, although on the plane of everyday life, African countries still struggle under outside authority); the hero, therefore, will not have to pit himself against an external obstacle, but against an inner one.

And that inner obstacle is an opportunity for Black African literature to renew itself.

In fact, the Black writer formerly struggled to rescue his race from the sorcery of the foreign school. And that anguished Black race asked itself this disturbing question: "Must we go to the West's school?" That is the question Oyono asked himself (*Houseboy, The Old Negro and the Medal*), and the question of

Cheikh Hamidou Kane (*Ambiguous Adventure*) and all the other writers who have asserted that the foreign school was only a lure. These writers did not understand, alas, that history is the best reference to the behavior of societies. They did not understand, or they understood only belatedly that centuries and societies develop in a direction that can be called unilateral, that history unfolds in irreversible fashion, regardless of what theoreticians of the philosophy of history think about it.

The historian Arnold Toynbee offers us a very eloquent diagram of the birth of societies, from antiquity to the modern era; he shows that all known civilizations have antecedents.

Modern Western civilization issued from Medieval Western civilization; the latter from Greco-Roman civilization, and that in turn from primitive society. In like manner, the Hindu, Chinese, and other civilizations have antecedents. Only the Egyptian civilization knew no antecedent.

Our race must, therefore, integrate itself with this stream and emerge from the modern technical world, unless it wants to relive its primitive existence, climbing unaided, groping along, out of the depths of obscurantism. And the fact is that Black writers chose the foreign school, although it was a lure for them (Camara Laye, Cheikh Hamidou Kane, etc.) for several reasons: the foreign school is a technique and the foreign school is an art.

How can one struggle effectively against foreign oppression if one does not know its technique and its art?

This is a question Alexis Stephen (Haitian) answers admirably in his novel, *The Musician Tree*. The hero, young Ganibo, who is to take the place of Bois d'Orme as chief of the Voodoo believers, becomes aware that religion is of no avail against modern forms of oppression, and that it is only in using the enemy's arms, his knowledge and his industry, that the Haitian people will give themselves the possibilities of regaining their full independence.

Alexis Stephen approves here the thought of Arnold Toynbee, which requires a civilization at grips with a stronger civilization to submit passively to the stronger civilization if it wants to survive, or to perish in its resistance. This has not been confirmed.

But the example the historian takes to shore up his assertion is compelling. He considers Russia at two decisive moments in its history. He asserts that until the thirteenth century Russia had permitted itself to be outdistanced by the West from the technical point of view. And not having wanted to accept Western technical civilization, it was unable to resist Western invaders from the thirteenth to the seventeenth centuries. Not until Peter the Great (czar from 1682 to 1721 and Russian emperor from 1721 to 1725) was the whole situation changed. Peter the Great, of course, opened Russia to Western civilization. He sent various Russians to the West to become acquainted with Western techniques. And that measure permitted the Russia that Peter the Great fashioned to resist the invasion of the Swedes in 1709, and of Napoleon in 1812.

But, Toynbee asks, is adapting the techniques of a civilization sufficient for fighting it effectively? Russia again serves as an example.

Russia understood that, to resist the West, she also had to penetrate the West's way of thinking. Thus she adopted a Western ideology, and applied it to the Russian system, after having shaken off Christianity, the fruit of Eastern evangelization from Byzantium. That ideology is communism, sprung from two German Westerners, Karl Marx and Friedrich Engels. And today Russia constitutes a serious threat to the West. Yet Russia uses no weapons other than those the West has made available, that is, techniques and an ideology, communism, which is evidently not what its initiators had conceived.

The concept Toynbee develops here is very bold. Yet it is shared unconsciously by certain of our Negro writers.

Grande Royale, in *The Ambiguous Adventure,* opens the country to the West so that tomorrow's Diallobes will know "every possible way to connect one piece of wood to another," and will learn the art of winning without being in the right. That is also the concept of Camara Laye and evidently of Alexis Stephen. It is, in short, that of all those writers who look to discussion and dialogue to show their nations the way to success.

CHAPTER 9:
physical death
of the hero

But isn't there danger in getting too close to one's enemy? Can the Black penetrate with impunity the thought and techniques of the West, the writers ask? The novelist who gives a vigorous and decisive answer to that question is Cheikh Hamidou Kane.

Probing an enemy and getting to know him is a perilous adventure. The West is a universe too different from ours to be approached without danger. When one makes the leap into it, the road back is often difficult to find. That universe never leaves those who venture into it untouched; it transforms them, metamorphoses them.

Samba Diallo, in *The Ambiguous Adventure*, deplores this situation when he declares, "When we leave home, we don't know if we will ever come back."

"We may be captured at the end of our journey, conquered by our venture itself. It suddenly appears to us that all along our road we never stopped undergoing change, and that we have become other than we were. Sometimes the metamorphosis is incomplete, and sets us down in a hybrid state and leaves us there. Then we go into hiding, filled with shame."

The Black African hero feels confusedly, therefore, that at the end of the adventure, at the close of his flirtation with the West, there is danger of death, spiritual death, because the hero does not find his way back again to the Black values of his ancestors.

He is like a young man who flirts with a girl, planning to leave her when he has no further need of her. But the girl, with the help of a magician, succeeds in clinging to the young man for life, through marriage. And the young man can only answer those who ask him to break away, to regain his freedom, by borrowing from Samba Diallo this hopeless reply: "I don't know whether one can ever find that road again when one has lost it" (that is, the road back to the heart of the free world).

"It's a case of the would-be taker being taken," La Fontaine would have said.

The hero wanted to take surreptitiously a bit of that flame which lights the road to the West in order to make use of it against the West, but he finds himself lured and caught like a fly.

Is this proof, once again, that Arnold Toynbee is right, when he declares that Western civilization is a whole, that one element of it cannot be adopted without all the others rushing in?

Is it true that the Black African hero who has made the leap to the West can no longer adapt to his native soil and to his original environment?

Is then the Black African's adventure in the West a divorce from his environment?

Here the question of the uprooted hero's return to his native soil is posed—the problem of the welcome his surroundings accord him; the problem of collaboration which the hero, who wants to put his roots down again, comes to offer his people; and the problem of the second death, the hero's physical death, as he becomes the victim of the destructive zeal of his own brothers.

Let us state immediately, in order to avoid any misunderstanding, that all the heros we will talk about are average people. There are no great politicians among them nor men of learning, except the hero of *The Ambiguous Adventure*, who has a degree in philosophy.

Let's mention them before discussing them: The hero of Ferdinand Oyono's *Houseboy* is a domestic servant (Toundi); the hero of Jacques Roumain's *Masters of the Dew* is a farm hand (Manuel); Chilembwe, the hero of Hans Hoffmeyer's *The Skin Is Deep,* also works on a farm. Camara Laye, the hero and author of *The Dark Child* is a school boy; Peter Abrahams, the hero of *I Am Not a Free Man,* is presented as a young man without schooling who is trying to make up on his own for his lack of education.

These heros are simple people. But that is only a symbol: the heros' modest condition signifies that Africa, an unproductive land up to that point, will produce in their hands delicious and abundant fruit. We shall divide these heros into two groups:

1. The heros who rushed off headlong to the West, and who came back rich in experience.

2. The heros who rushed off headlong to the West to acquire knowledge and did not return.

The first group is divided into three subgroups, and poses a triple problem, which we will examine by stages.

All these heros will die; and it is the meaning of this physical death which interests us.

The first subgroup is represented by Toundi, the hero of *Houseboy*.

The story unfolds before the independence of Cameroon. Toundi is a little boy who becomes a victim of his curiosity, of which he has too much. The West had opened its doors wide to him; but the impatient little boy wants to penetrate the secret of the West very quickly, and he is crushed by the foreign weight before he has had time to grasp anything whatever of this Western mirage. He belongs, therefore to the category of those violent heros that we mentioned earlier, and whom we will not study in depth, because that period soon passed and no longer offers much interest from a literary point of view, except perhaps to those who always want to create new opportunities for confusion, or who build up out of proportion inconsequential events to justify inhuman misconduct.

The second subgroup is comprised of heros shaped by the West, who, despite the metamorphosis they have undergone, decided to return home, to bring their contribution to the great building that constitutes the Black world, that building which colonization started and that the Africans themselves must complete. They are represented by Samba Diallo, the hero of *Ambiguous Adventure.*

But as soon as this hero had come back under the paternal roof, he was assassinated by a madman.

This hero was the object of a very lively debate among the Chief Teacher of the Diallobes, the Chief of the Diallobes and Grande Royale.

This hero, who had to go and learn "all the other ways to fasten one board to another," and "the art of winning without being in the right," is struck down without having time to reveal even a scrap of the Western secrets.

He is accused of having forgotten too much, of having perhaps forgotten the essential: he no longer knows how to pray.

Unlike Toundi, the hero of Ferdinand Oyono, he is killed not by the West, but by Africa itself a too exacting Africa, exacting to the point of proposing to one of its sons, Samba Diallo, the alternative of death or obedience to the stipulated order.

This is the disagreeable situation the Black African novel foresees, a situation which has a chance of becoming characteristic of relations between Africans themselves.

But this is a game and Africa is the losing player, unable to find the good side of the medal that was Samba Diallo; Africa sees only the wrong side.

What is disturbing is not so much Samba Diallo's death. We are accustomed to this type of death as a result of disobedience; we saw much of it under colonialism, under the form of official executions, or of assassinations carried out by the militia man obeying an administrator's secret orders. What disturbs us is the fact that the assassination is the work of Africa itself.

Must we believe that history repeats itself? Fortunately, what happens in the novel doesn't exactly happen in life. The fact remains that we address our most constructive reproaches to that fictional and intolerant Africa: Samba Diallo hardly returns, hardly settles down before he becomes the object of a spiritual and moral search. Violent Africa erupts around him, drags him from under his father's roof to destroy him like a dog, near the tomb of the Diallobes' Chief Teacher. Samba Diallo forgot, that is a fact; he refused to pray, that is true. Yet isn't his death more damaging for the Diallobes than his forgetfulness and his disobedience which were only momentary?

The shadows cover everything; but this shadow also fills the hearts of the Diallobes, and it was prophetic.

The third subgroup includes heros shaped by the West who return enriched by experience and have time to breathe into the ears of a few fortunate ones the mystery of the West. They are represented by Manuel, the hero of *Masters of the Dew*.

But here a difficulty also arises: the multiplicity of languages which confuse everything. The problem is that in the little society of Fonds-Rouge where Manuel, on his return from Cuba, wants to sink his roots again, several more or less rational, more or less emotional languages are spoken.

Fonds-Rouge is rent by misery, because a severe dry spell is crushing the country: animals, men, and plants are dying. If this society is to live, it must speak a single language: the language of love and of work. But confusion reigns in Fonds-Rouge, as formerly in Babel, and as in some of our societies.

What languages do they speak there?

The language of the straw man: The straw man is represented by Hilarion, the rural police officer who takes advantage of the people's misery to sell at usurious prices the bit of food the region still produces or that he imports, because only he can afford to do so.

He will be the first to oppose Manuel when Manuel tries to improve the living conditions of the people. Because his interests are threatened if Manuel succeeds, Hilarion, the symbol of the straw men that are found in our societies, treats Manuel as a rebel; in our society Hilarion would call him a counter-revolutionary. He threatens to paralyze Manuel's social action in trying to bring water to Fonds-Rouge.

The language of the meek: Those who believe that all is over, since God, who is the creator of all, has permitted misery in society. These are Bien-Aimé and Délira-Délivrance, Manuel's parents, and Annaise, his fiancee.

And Manuel's social action finds in them a serious obstacle: he will literally have to wear himself out to persuade them that by saying a big "no" to resignation, and a big "yes" to work, they will repulse misery.

The language of the fainthearted: This is the language of those who think that when the situation deteriorates inside, remedies can come only from outside.

This is the case of Joachin and of Destiné who shamelessly abandon their ancestral land to go to other lands in search of a living, when they should have taken care of their own, in order to make it produce the fruits essential to life.

Jacques Roumain denounces here, with much finesse, those young underdeveloped countries, which, taking advantage of their condition, seek outside financing for even the most elementary economic improvements—those which would require only a low national investment. Often those countries called underdeveloped, to which the novelist is addressing himself here, are made up only of numerous delegations that they send abroad to negotiate for help they rarely get, delegations which incur expenses in amounts that would have paid for several appreciable economic improvements.

Manuel has to stifle the tendency of his fellow citizens to count too much on help from others.

The language of the irresponsible, of the jealous: Here is Gervilien, the man without faith, who asks only to settle an old score at the expense of the national cause.

Manuel must, therefore, put this language in the shade in order to teach his fellow citizens the language of reason, of love and of work.

But challenged by so many native enemies, Manuel will be overcome.

He will harvest trouble: the police will not pardon him.

He will endure mistrust: his good faith will be questioned, and his healthful projects not accepted. He will be known only as the man who came back from Cuba—from the West (Cuba before Fidel Castro is meant here).

He will therefore be misunderstood and very few people will take advantage of his experience: these will be the ones who you might say are in the state of grace. They accept the counsels of salvation. These are Manuel's parents; Annaise, his fiancee; and his friends, Larivoire and Laurelien. The others believe that his moderation is cowardice. They push Manuel to revenge, to selfish actions. Such a hero, too far ahead of his society, often finds very few people who understand him.

So many enemies combined against a single man, so much bitter spittle spewed on the face of the misunderstood hero, shorten his life. He, like Samba Diallo, is the victim of the violence of an unrestrainable fanatic. He is destroyed at night, like a defenseless dog, for pure souls have no defense but their simplicity.

The two heros we have just considered have been rejected by their surroundings. Misunderstood and objects of mistrust on the part of the people, they have been denied by their own. We can apply to these heros the words of Holy Scripture about the liberator: "He went to his own, and his own received him not."

CHAPTER 10:
alienation or misunderstanding

Is the hero definitely alienated from his surroundings? Or does the separation amount to nothing more than a temporary misunderstanding?

We should point out, before answering that question, that the assassins of these heros are madmen—men who have lost control of their feelings, permanently (Samba Diallo's assassin), or momentarily under the effect of anger (Gervilien, Manuel's assassin). They act violently and brutishly because their reason is unable to triumph. They are, then, not responsible; and their actions are not approved by the intelligent and thoughtful men of their societies.

Moreover, one of their assassins will end up by running away; he will become aware that his violence, far from elevating him above the people, resulted only in pitting all the others against him, because they understood that he was motivated only by ambition. He wanted to found his house on a land watered by the blood of those he could ward off by violence. For violence, that destructive violence, is the instrument of the weak. All who preach it and resort to it are weak men; they are troubled men who are afraid of losing. The man who is strong within himself is a calm man who knows that if he is misunderstood today, tomorrow he will perhaps be acknowledged to be in the right. While waiting, he will try to understand the others in order to make them understand. To convince ourselves of this, we have only to compare the behavior of the madmen— the assassin of Samba Diallo and the assassin of Manuel—and the behavior of Samba Diallo and Manuel themselves.

The first two are restless, troubled, gnawed by jealousy, undermined by the feeling that they can do nothing against their enemy without using cowardly means: assassination. Their attitude is also cowardly, because after the assassination they lack the courage to admit their deed.

The second two, the victims, are characterized by an extraordinary calm, the assurance that the condition of the salvation of their people is reconciliation—general pardon granted without bargaining. Manuel, unruffled, will seek that reconciliation even at the cost of his own blood. For him, reconciliation is neither surrender nor defeat, but the result of understanding, of constructive awareness.

In his great desire to see reconciliation accomplished, Manuel, before giving up the ghost, even forbids his mother to denounce his assassin, Gervilien. For if Gervilien is denounced, the quarrel will rekindle and prevent reconciliation, without which the social and economic development of Fonds-Rouge would be impossible.

Gervilien, foolish and stupid, thought after the blow that no one knew who was responsible. But those most closely affected knew it: Manuel's mother, his fiancee Annaise, his friends Laurelien and Larivoire and many others.

Yet to the great astonishment of the assassin, those entrusted with the secret remained silent in favor of reconciliation. This was the greatest defeat that the inhabitants of Fonds-Rouge inflicted on Gervilien, the partisan of violence. This is the proof that violence is only a temporary measure that every society will denounce and eliminate sooner or later. And Manuel is amply avenged, by gentleness, by the inhabitants of Fonds-Rouge themselves. What he had worked for, reconciliation, will be achieved after his death, and drought will be permanently conquered.

Since the hero will be recognized as a true savior, it is not a question of a divorce, but simply of a misunderstanding which will be cleared up one day, even after the hero's death. For the people's judgment is infallible, even if belated.

And that hero whom we had thought rejected, will save his nation. That salvation will take place in stages:

The Black African hero is a conciliator: A nation that wants to put itself together cannot do so as long as it is divided and full of hate. The inhabitants of

Fonds-Rouge are animated by a feeling of revenge, for an old quarrel sets some against others.

Fonds-Rouge is therefore a house divided against itself and it cannot struggle effectively against the outside enemy, the drought.

Fonds-Rouge could be in this a symbol of our nations: they can build themselves up only in unity. Or it could be a symbol of all Africa, which can be a great continent only in harmony.

To attain this goal, then, Manuel preaches reconciliation. Reconciliation is the essential condition for love among the inhabitants, and love is the one condition for the prosperity of the country.

This hero is the organizer of the great coumbite (which means "collective farm work"). For only the great *coumbite* will be able to bring water as far as the plain. It is synonymous with unity.

Manuel will be, then, thanks to the methods learned in the foreign school, the organizer of the great *coumbite,* of the work which will give back to each individual his place in the community.

Manuel refuses to compromise with his conscience and his duty. He must not, then, compromise with his family, which advises him not to associate the other families in the social and economic construction of Fonds-Rouge. He refuses to come to terms with those who encourage him to seek revenge. Because his uncle Sauveur has been killed in a brawl, Manuel is, according to custom, supposed to avenge his humiliated family. But the hero refuses to be a new Orso, and Jacques Roumain a new Merimée. No Corsican-style vendetta in *Masters of the Dew*. Everything about Manuel is pure.

To compromise with his conscience, to come to terms with his milieu which is torn by hatred, revenge, and ambition, to accept responsibility for a continually destructive vendetta, is to give the enemy outside the opportunity to strengthen his position and to win without striking a blow.

Now, the most terrible enemy that threatens the little region of Fonds-Rouge is the economic misery caused by the great drought that prevents the seeds from germinating. Manuel therefore requests the inhabitants of Fonds-Rouge to stand up to that terrible enemy, economic misery, to stem it, like a sickness, by the most appropriate treatment. And Manuel is convinced that the economic drought will be conquered, that both physical and spiritual water will return to Fonds-Rouge. Nor is he disturbed about the clash with Gervilien, the madman. He rejoices at the thought that most of the community is finally going to agree to fight the drought with him; the others, those who still hesitate to accept his ideas, will be won over by the water when it begins to flow again. It would, therefore, be very clumsy of Manuel to want at this stage to convince Gervilien by force.

According to Jacques Roumain, therefore, the hero who has made a leap into the West is not necessarily lost to the Black world. If this hero returns to his own people, and if he is not a madman, there is no divorce.

CHAPTER 11:
spiritual death
of the hero

This leads us directly to the second big group: those heros who made a leap into the West and did not come back; those who are victims of the Western mirage, and who are dead as far as the Negro world is concerned. Their death is spiritual; they made no resistance to their metamorphosis, and have, therefore, definitely lost the road back to the heart of the African world, that road Cheikh Hamidou Kane speaks of in *The Ambiguous Adventure.*

These heros who did not come back are represented by Camara Laye and Peter Abrahams.

Camara Laye, hero and author of *The Dark Child,* after having resisted the attraction of the foreign school, let himself be carried away without hope of return.

Camara Laye's promises to his father and to his sweetheart Marie nevertheless seemed firm. "Promise me that you will come back some day," his father demanded. "I'll come back!" Camara Laye assured him.

And little Marie was disturbed too: "You'll come back?" she asked. "Yes," the traveller replied laconically.

But we wait in vain for the hero of *The Dark Child* to return to Guinea. Camara Laye's novel remains open, or, as one would say, hanging. The faint hope we still have of seeing this novel close fades away. And this open novel, this "dark child," this Black hero gone off forever to the West, disturbs us. The Black world is disturbed about it because it means that the Black world, suspended with its hero, is an eternal question mark for that world itself. And it means, moreover, that Black Africa does not know how to formulate its problems, and consequently is unable to delimit them in order to try to solve them.

These open novels and these suspended heros pose the initial question correctly but do not even glimpse the final question; they leave the Black world in uncertainty at the very beginning of its course.

Through the disquiet that his suspended novel creates, Camara Laye suggests a question: "Where are we going? Where is the Black world going?"

But Jacques Roumain, through his closed novel, was able to define what the Black world faces. He knows what this disinherited world should want: life. And throughout his life Manuel, his hero, asked himself and tried to answer the following question:

"What conditions are necessary for the Black to live fully?"

Manuel proves by the answer he gives to that question that the old myth of "mysterious" Africa should be allowed to collapse. If Black Africa is still a mystery to the foreigner, to Blacks who have delimited its problems, all has become clear.

Perhaps Camara Laye senses in a confused way the fate Black Africa reserves for his hero. Might I suggest that this Africa—still enveloped in the pungent atmosphere of the forests, and close to her ancestral spirits, but at the same time impatient to solve the problems of the moment—often fails to understand those of her children who have gone to a foreign school and do not think as she does. Perhaps Camara Laye senses unfortunate consequences for his hero—similar to the consequences that the madman and Gervilien respectively reserved for Samba Diallo and Manuel.

Perhaps he also senses that because he himself is the hero of his novel, his real life and the one he leads within the confines of his book would diverge, if he ended the book by having his hero return to Guinea—as he had promised his father he would do in order to tell him about his leap into the West.

African literature often reveals to Blacks only one of its many faces, the war against the foreign school. Here we have an aspect of it that Blacks forget very quickly: a man's greatest enemies are the people of his own household.

By presenting to us heros grappling not only with imperialism, but also with their own brothers,

Black African writers urge us to ask ourselves if
sometimes we are the ones who are holding back the
social, political, and economic impetus of our own
countries.

Who should be condemned if the Black African
hero, rich with experiences of value to the Black
world, is misunderstood and rejected on his return
from the West—despite his wish to involve himself
once again in the life of the village?

Who should be condemned? The Blacks
themselves, including the hero. If they had surpassed
themselves, they would have sacrificed their petty
interests to the benefit of the general interest.

Who should be condemned, if certain heros of
Black African literature have been completely
fascinated by the mirage of the West which killed
them spiritually?

Who should be condemned? Once again, it is the
Blacks themselves who are blameworthy; it is the
heros who understood nothing of their mission. If the
foreign school takes us captive, it is because it
depends on our own weakness.

And those Black writers who take up the
national cause invite us to courageously strike our
breasts and admit: "From such a time in history to
such a time in history we ourselves were the artisans
of our own national lack of balance." Black African
writers reveal to us that our responsibility has no
limit, that we are dishonest and hardly sincere with
ourselves if we always blame others for what has
resulted from our own weakness.

PART IV:
reflections

CHAPTER 12:
defining
a black culture

We have long been faced with the agonizing question: is there a valid African or Black African civilization?

The answer, often emotional, varies according to the side one is on. But men of Black African culture, putting aside emotional aspects, have examined history. Thus has been born in them, over a little more than thirty years, a clear awareness of a culture, of an autonomous Black African civilization.

But that awareness, despite the good fortune of *négritude* and the establishment of the institution known as *Présence Africaine,* has remained too individual: should it have arisen for all Blacks alike? Who should take the responsibility?

That mission had been entrusted (and it is still so entrusted) to the West. Unfortunately, the West (perhaps through overzealousness?) has contributed only to shaping the African Black to its own image, when it was being asked, at the same time it was revealing the Black to other worlds, to reveal him also and especially to himself.

This is what Edouard Maunique calls the practice of the philosophy of identification. The "Europe of good will" wanted the Black world to look like it; and it said to the pupil "Look at me," when it should have been saying "Look at yourself, examine yourself."

But the order from such an exalted source was respected: The Black African looked so long and so well at the master that he forgot who he was, where he came from, and where he was going.

If the Black had been able to identify completely with his master, there would have been no problem. Unfortunately, that identification was imperfect, incomplete: the Black, coming out of himself, was unable to integrate fully with Western civilization; in the future he will be neither like himself nor like the other; he is a hybrid, the very one illustrated by Cheikh Hamidou Kane's *Ambiguous Adventure*.

We will not say, however, that Europe failed in its mission; it simply has not reached its goal, although it tried. It must now be relieved by Black Africans themselves. They know better than Europe the shortcuts, the fords, the passes, which will allow them to reach their goal after a creditable effort, without cheating and without too much delay.

Thus the Black himself has seized the rudder and will steer his cultural bark. This is, moreover, what the humanitarian West has always desired. But the Black wants first of all to make certain that the vessel contains a treasure. It is therefore to look at itself, to make an inventory of its possessions, that the Black African group, aided by available Westerners, gathered at Dakar.

In order to discover itself, this group addressed a question to itself: "Have I been capable of creation?" —that is, "Am I capable of giving to the world, as I have received from the world?" In order to answer this question it is necessary to examine the way the soul of a people expresses itself, to examine its artistic creations. Two other questions inseparable from the first then appear.

Is there a specifically Black culture, that is to say, a typically Black soul?

Does Black culture perform a function in the life of the Black peoples?

Let us say immediately, with Aimé Césaire, that there is first of all art itself, universal art; and Black culture is only a particular aspect of that art, as is Western art or Oriental art. They all cooperate in the production of *universal civilization*. And it is to make certain that the Black world is present when the civilization of the universe takes shape, declared Lamine Gueye, president of the Senegalese Parliament, that the Conference on the Art of the Black World was convened in the mid-1960's as a forum for Blacks to make an introspective examination. Such an examination is necessary as we have said, because those entrusted with saving us have made of us only imperfect images of themselves, because their past, different from ours, imposes on them a certain way of seeing and of judging.

As a matter of fact, examination of Black culture, and therefore of the Black soul and mind, was until recently the domain of Europeans alone. They dictated to the world a way of interpreting Black culture, a method of investigation that was often not exempt from prejudice, their past, and their education, obliging them until very recently to judge Black art in the framework of a classical and overly rigid typology. "In the name of a certain unity of art," says Lamine Dialokite, "we have witnessed an attempt to reduce everything to the same level." The authenticity of Black art was disappearing because the West looked upon it with the same eyes it used for its own art or for Greek and Roman art. Black art remained simply a museum piece, its meaning and significance possessing no value in Western eyes. Europe, seeing only the esthetic and architectural aspect of Black art, was ignorant of its conceptual and functional side.

The Conference therefore gave itself a mission: to reassert the role of Black art, that of translating the Black soul and strengthening Black awareness among all Blacks, not in a racial concept, but simply in a national sense, so that the Black world would also have its own identity, and so that Africa would truly erect its own structure.

Two important individuals defined the meaning of the Conference as follows:

André Malraux, representing General de Gaulle and western culture, stated that he was entrusted with bringing to the Conference the message of a West conscious of the complementary quality of human values, complementarity which requires the contributions of others and the respect of others. We will return frequently to these points.

For Senghor, the Conference translated into action the fidelity of Blacks to Africa. Therefore this Conference was one of *négritude.*

Since construction of the Black world by Blacks conscious of the "necessary complementarity" was the essential theme of the Conference, it is fitting to now examine the idea of *négritude.* In broad terms *négritude* means that which pertains to the Black race.

There has been, of course, much faultfinding with the concept of *négritude.* Hundreds of works have already proposed a thousand and one definitions which surround the concept with evergrowing uncertainty. But it is nonetheless true for the Black man that the concept of *négritude* includes both a demand and an affirmation of his presence, of his place in the concert of civilizations. That definition especially is one that the Conference retained because it includes all the others. The West has often criticized this concept. It has said, first of all, that the term was poorly chosen. Phonetically speaking, it does, perhaps, sound odd to the ear; but it is not more dissonant than long accepted words, such as aptitude, attitude, longitude, latitude, whose phonological composition is the same.

If its semantic content is complex and bothersome, that, far from making the expression detestable, only translates what has always been the case—that is to say, that the Black world was obscure and inaccessible and will remain so as long as it is not defined in politico-economic and socio-cultural human terms as the West has been.

The expression *négritude* is therefore neither vague nor imprecise. It translates a state, a way-of-being of a race. And perhaps one of its most eloquent meanings is precisely in the ardent desire of Blacks conscious of belonging to themselves; in their fear of being defrauded, deprived of themselves; in the watchfulness they impose on themselves to prevent their being surprised out of their entity.

That fear took shape in a marginal Black, a Black of the Islands, who cried out from the rostrum, "I will stand watch not an hour, but all my life, so that my son, a marginal Negro like me, may grasp the very essence of our life." The speaker was Edouard Maunique, who by such a declaration restores confidence.

Barely a few decades ago all half-breeds called themselves White (in the Congo, at least). Today they are all Black. That proves to us that salvation is always possible.

Indeed, Edouard Maunique and all other marginal Blacks sought and found again the better part of their lives, and now it will never be taken from them. That is what they have begun to reveal to themselves. That revelation, or rather, that resurrection was brought about through the medium of authentic Black art.

"Black art is not wax," Edouard Maunique proclaims proudly. It is not wax, it is rather a flame that collects, that attracts, as in the evening in Black villages the flame of the common hearth calls all Blacks.

All Blacks who are aware of themselves are now consumed by the fear of not being black enough. Many writers have treated this theme in poetry.

A Ghanaian poet, Ernest Kobina Parkes, presents this anxiety to us through the expression of Black souls. (See his poem "African Heaven")

Another poet expresses the attachment of discerning Blacks to the Black race and their pride in that race in the form of a supplication; he asks the painter to bring him, not the morning sun, but the night sun, that is, the sun that is plunged in darkness, that is black. This is another symbol. And in his poem entitled "Black Suns" the poet J. P. Kindamba says:

> Bring me the evening sun
> The setting sun, the night sun
> The sun that flows and sinks.
> Bring me the sun that sleeps
> Or drowses; the sun that is engulfed;
> The sun that drowns and forgets itself.
> Bring me the sun that murmurs;
> The sun that sighs, the sun that moans;
> The sun that weeps and wails.
> Painter, bring me, oh painter
> The sun that dies in the evening;
> The sun that is dying at dusk.

Morning sun! Sun that bursts open!
Sun that breaks through! Sun that is born!
No! That is life! And I hate life.
Bring me the sun that glows.
The sun bursting in the African sky,
At the black hours when the tattoo is sounded.
Bring me the restful sun:
After the morning labors, the daily effort;
When the completed work fades in memory.
Bring me, oh painter! Bring me, painter,
The parting sun, the sun of death,
In the evening of my earthly journey.

Can that anguish of Blacks aware that they do not belong to their race be better expressed?

It is also claimed that the term *négritude* is restrictive and racist. *Négritude,* declared a member of the Conference, must open its horizons, so that those who are not Black, but who may find in *négritude* an opportunity to live, may enrich themselves, may deepen their own humanity.

Has *négritude* ever closed its doors? *Négritude* may be the affirmation of Black humanity, but it is not restrictive. Its goal is precisely to meet all men and all civilizations at the summit.

There are Blacks who have found in Western civilization an opportunity to enrich their own humanity; why should the West be refused the chance to enrich itself in contact with the rediscovered Black world? All Westerners are welcome—especially those who unearth our past, so rich in teachings, who revive and establish standards for our endangered dialects, and who guide our first faltering steps as apprentice researchers.

These will deepen their own knowledge and enrich us. That is, in part, what the great Malraux calls *necessary complementarity;* indispensable complementarity, he might better have said.

Thus, there is nothing restrictive about the concept of *négritude.* There is nothing racist in it either. It would be a stupid racism which would stifle our Black life, which is barely awakening. The expression refers only, as we shall see presently, (and we rely here upon the authority of Alioune Diop) to the historic accident which gave Blacks a "special" place in history.

The Conference calmed anxieties, and in accord with the author of *Man's Fate,* recommended close collaboration with other civilizations. Each, of course, will keep its own distinctive hallmarks, and welcome others with respect and dignity.

The Black race welcomed Europe, said the editor of *Présence Africaine;* how would it not be happy and proud to give, in turn, the best it has within itself? For, regardless of what may be said, he continued, there is a Black civilization that must be revealed to the world under the most favorable conditions.

A certain group has even wanted to contrast *négritude,* the term in use among French speakers, and the expression "African personality," the expression preferred by English speakers.

One senses that certain ill-intentioned Western Africanists have worked out two sociological systems, one applicable in the former English colonies, the other in the former French colonies. They want to divide these two parts—which actually form one body—in order to keep the Black world weak.

But other Africanists have discovered that even though the two groups have undergone two different educational processes, their heart is still one. They are Blacks who have long been scorned, long likened to objects for sale. And unanimously the members of the Conference, Black Africans and Westerners, rejected the quarrel over terminology as absurd and leading nowhere. For what gave birth to the concept expressed in two different ways remains the same: the desire of the Black world to cope with the humiliating situation the civilized world imposed on it, the situation that Alioune Diop called very delicately "an historic accident."

Therefore, the question is to defend and illustrate Black cultural values, to assert them, to assert the Black continent and the Black world, and to survive. There is no contrast between the two expressions, but simply diversity in expressing the same concept and the same ideal.

Finally, it has been said that as a concept *négritude* is old-fashioned and out-of-date, that on the whole it has outlived its time. That is disturbing, especially when one hears Aimé Césaire proclaim loftily to the Conference: "I don't like the word *négritude* at all"—Césaire, one of the recognized creators of the concept.

But let us not be misled. Maybe Césaire does not like the word simply because it puts him too much in the public eye, just as certain Blacks do not like to have a nose that is too flat because it draws everyone's attention to them. But that doesn't change in the least the fact that the flat nose is real.

Aimé Césaire, who is also representative from Martinique to the French National Assembly, understood this, moreover, so well that he hastened to defend the word, stating in his lecture closing the work of the Conference, "The expression *négritude* has its good points and its bad; but it is abused and distorted; it must be vindicated by reference to the situation of Blacks at the time of its birth between 1930 and 1940."

If the notion of *négritude* was born, it was because from some point on, the Black man was no longer reached by the White man, Césaire declares. Was this because the Black soul is inaccessible? Was it a deliberate effort not to translate the reality? In any case, it is agreed that the White man replaced the authentic Black with a caricature, a series of prejudices, an image deformed by Western processes.

It was necessary that the first Black poets rise against that humiliating situation at any price. Thus was born the literature of *négritude,* which rehabilitates the Black man "in his original stature."

This rehabilitation is a combat, a claiming back. But if the battle of revindication is won, is the war over?

Africa is still struggling, more than ever, against the outside, but especially against Africa herself. There are still too many who are unconscious; among them are thousands of new arrivals, profiteers, who seize on the present situation and not knowing the price of a victory dearly won, lure the people on toward misty horizons full of snares in the name of a supposed equality. Through literature Black African men of culture have revealed to the forces of colonization the existence of an authentic and inalienable Negro personality. These same men, more numerous today, must now undertake a dialogue with their fellow citizens, so that the latter will analyze themselves better than they have done thus far. They must be helped to see where they are coming from, where they are going, and signs that mark their way.

In a word, may Black African men of culture, through dialogue, lead their fellow citizens to ask themselves if they are faithful to Africa, or if they have repudiated her most sacred human values.

CHAPTER 13:
dialogue

The Conference on Art of the Black World was concerned primarily with launching a frank dialogue among its members: a dialogue among Black Africans and a dialogue between Black Africans and others.

This exchange played a determining role in the development of the Conference and in its success. In this process the Conference followed the route of the poets of *négritude*. Indeed, as we have already said, *négritude* chose to approach other men indirectly, through poetry. White men listened to the song of the poet, in which they recognized fragments of thinking humanity. They answered; and thus a dialogue between the West and the Black world was born, the peaceful weapon which "restored the Black man to his original stature," according to Aimé Césaire. "There is no true dialogue between a man and a thing," he added.

The Conference and the Dakar Festival of Black Arts are proof that the Black has climbed a step higher, that his Western brother is holding out a helping hand to him so that in the spirit of *necessary complementarity* he can climb still higher and help him at last to see what was kept from his eyes before the dialogue was born. For the real community is cultural in nature. Here objectivity is possible; elsewhere it is emotionalism, selfishness, pride, and scorn that reign. But in order for accord to be possible, dialogue must exist. That is what the representative of Western Culture and of General de Gaulle put into words at the opening of the Conference when he said, "Cultural community is possible only through dialogue."

Nevertheless, if dialogue makes a community possible, it does not do so automatically; community exists only when there is a contribution of the groups composing it. The Black African group, recognized henceforth as a thinking participant, wants to contribute its share to the common table, to the table where the model of the modern world, the convergence of all civilizations, is taking shape.

But in that community, the Black world wants to remain itself; it has so long been defrauded of its identity that in no case and under no circumstances will it consent to wear a mask. It wants to be seen as it is and to be helped by the Western world to become aware of its shortcomings.

Thus by being sincere with themselves, Black African men of culture achieved a dialogue that Black politicians have been incapable of bringing about, although they have steeped us every day in mawkish declarations made in the name of humanity and understanding among men. Too selfish, too jealous of their power, and unceasingly fearful of losing it, they always suspect malevolent intent in all those who make a desperate effort to establish a human dialogue with them. And we are proud to find for an instant, in the midst of an unbiased gathering, our Senghor, who, alas, becomes a politician again when it pleases him.

We wish that the Dakar event will be a lesson of human significance for them. Dialogue rescued Black African culture by rescuing Black art, which, in turn, will repersonalize the Black by revitalizing his contact with himself and with other civilizations—by making him sense again what he can become. Then the politician will again find mature citizens, reflective, well educated, open to national and to Black Negro impulses, and to the rhythmical beat of the modern world.

But as long as Black politicians are faced with collaborators and citizens without cultural education, without open minds, without knowledge of the soul of their race, and therefore without possibility of foreseeing the problems that can arise at the level of the people, these politicians, and this is certain, will rely on the unthinking, who howl in the streets for an opportunity for life, but who do not believe the ideas they proclaim and the slogans that they trumpet in the public square.

That is what the poet from Martinique announced in other terms at the close of the

Conference when he said (we summarize): If Black African statesmen ask us, men of culture, to educate the Black people, to open their minds, to make men of them, we will answer them: statesmen, politicians, make good policies for us, African policies, and art will be saved and the citizens will be enlightened.

The Conference has, indeed, seen that the absence of dialogue with others is an indication of lack of maturity or, on the cultural, political, and social level, of a dictatorial mind.

The Black man of culture, together with Westerners of good will, having given the Black world an awareness of itself by liberating it from imposed culture, recognizes that the war is not over. Struggles, perhaps more difficult, remain to be undertaken. Black intellectuals and friends must undertake the beneficial dialogue with their own people and with one another.

The Black African has questioned the West about his condition. He must now question himself. This was one of the chief ideas of the Conference; for, even if colonization has disappeared in most of the Black countries, the danger of the disintegration of Black culture and conscience has not been averted. This is the opinion of Aimé Césaire who says that to be valid the shield of political independence must be reinforced by the shield of an art freed from all outside constraint.

We will permit ourselves here to paraphrase a well-known writer and say: political independence without a national and cultural consciousness expresses very little.

The Black must therefore converse with himself as well as with others; he must draw up the balance sheet of his cultural movement and examine his possibilities for survival.

But should the necessity of interior dialogue lead the Black world to reject the help the West makes available? Or should the Black's dialogue with himself make the West, foreign to Black culture, undertake the simple role of catalyst?

To develop while at the same time remaining itself, Black art should reinvigorate itself through its own roots. But it also needs the help of other civilizations. Perhaps certain of their methods, when these are truly in the service of humanity, can help Black art and culture find themselves again. What precious catalysts Black artists would find there! But only these artists are in a position to choose the Western methods that are capable of helping our art to personalize itself again. In other words, no directive of a purely political nature is valid in such a case.

It must be honestly confessed, however, that the West is not always a simple catalyst. We know that specifically Black art has, at a given moment, gotten away from those who fashioned it, because of the regrettable "historical accident" which perverted the Black, making him take the road to Europe. It is therefore by way of Europe that thousands of artists and Black men of culture: writers, poets, musicians, sculptors, painters, architectural designers, comedians, etc., come back to their own civilization. They went to the West's school; and as we have said, many of them came back enriched with new experiences for the benefit of Black civilization.

Therefore, as Francis Bebey of Cameroon so rightly emphasized, it is not a regrettable thing to go through the West to find Black art once again; by passing along Europe's road, we Blacks have covered our feet with gold dust which allows us to fashion, with our own material, our jewel, a jewel specifically Black.

But many Blacks, flaunting a smug nationalism and doing violence to their intellectual honesty, deny any contribution of the West to the revitalization of Black art. They do not realize that Malraux's "necessary complementarity" is more than a rule of conduct; it is a law. Such Blacks, misled by a blind chauvinism, must begin with themselves the salutary dialogue which will help them see the light.

Another question that artists and cultured Blacks must put to themselves in their interior dialogue is this: Has Negro art jettisoned all its values? Has it nothing left to transmit to the world?

Blacks and Westerners assembled at Dakar, looking closely at themselves, answered: Nothing has yet been said: Black culture and art are only at the beginning of its mission, which is to make Blacks aware of their special place in history and to reveal to other civilizations a civilization long scorned and depersonalized, although as authentic and as old as humanity. And Malraux declared, "Africa has started off on the adventure of creation, and adventure is greatness." The minister should have perhaps added that it is not a question this time of an "ambiguous adventure," but of a conscious and resolute march toward the past and the future performed in the present. A march toward the past, because Blacks must convince themselves they were not what the racists said they were—nothing but savages stuffing themselves with the flesh of their fellows. A march toward the future: they must study if they are to be other than simple consumers of civilizations. Will they themselves never produce? A very disturbing question, but one that Alioune Diop answers with much optimism.

Actually there are forces working in the Black world that we can count on. The very forces which struggled for Black political independence must now band together to build Africa. And, according to Alioune Diop, intellectuals must be the craftsmen that guide the Black peoples in that task. Despite the fierce determination of certain individuals to humiliate them before their own race, intellectuals are the cornerstone of the Black edifice.

Unfortunately, these intellectuals often do not know how to begin so grandiose an enterprise. Because of pride or lack of information they have never approached Black peoples and their art, which has remained for them an art of the minority. This art, however, has been characterized as "art of the depths, the Black art called suffering, the joy of the man of Africa, with the gravity and pathos that characterizes him."

Give a little attention to sculpture, to painting, to traditional music in even a small city like Brazzaville, and you will learn how the forms, the attitudes, and the very words communicate a whole way of life.

Pride and ignorance work together to break down the Black concept of art. But there *is* a Black concept of art. There is in general an ideal relation between art and society; and in the Black world much more than elsewhere, the work draws its significance from its relationship with the environment that produced it—its relationship with the tribe, to be precise. Unfortunately, that relationship is in the process of being lost in Africa, just as it was lost in Western civilization long ago.

It is that loss that Black intellectuals want to avoid, or at least to delay. This calls for the coordination of all who are involved in the task. But their disparity is very great.

On the side of Western humanists and Africanists a glimmer of hope has appeared: the race of self-proclaimed researchers is over—"researchers" who used to fly from city to city, from Paris, London, or elsewhere, from the Cape of Good Hope by way of Dakar, Brazzaville, etc., returning to the West, after two months of soaring at twenty thousand feet above the savages, to give lectures entitled "Here is Today's Africa."

No, you amateur researchers! You are imposters and you disfigure Africa by mutilating it. Fortunately your type is dying, killed by its own shame. We now have true Africanists; they come and spend

two, four, six, ten, fifteen, even twenty years; why
not? It is a long and difficult time for them. For since
the approach is not always direct, they must proceed
by way of translation which is always in some small
way a betrayal.

Nevertheless these Western Africanists find
Blacks "who live, work, think and create in the
framework of their environment," says the Western
scholar William Fagg. These artists are able to
appreciate their art, because it is a function of their
belief. Unfortunately, they do not have the means of
preserving its original essence, and they lack
possibilities of development. This is where the
problem of the protection of the artist comes in.

CHAPTER 14:
a plea for the artist
and his works

In the Black African world in general little care is taken to give artists and works of art the place they deserve. There is only the individual artist; he has no diploma, and is penniless to boot. And very few Africans suspect the spiritual authority of Guy Léon Fylla, the painter, of Grégoire Massengo, the sculptor, of Joachim Massamba, the ceramist, of Antoine Moundanda, the traditional musician, of Guy Menga, the playwright, or of Marius Yelolo, the actor who can portray so well the king of Koka-Mbala.

Who troubles himself about their education?

Who troubles himself about the work of the researcher who tries by every means to determine the time and place of a particular aspect of Congolese life?

149

These artists and these researchers go un-heralded. Some of them often can't eat until their neighbors, if they have a heart, give them a little rice—and that is the literal truth.

The artist is a wise man, a seer. He is charged with making revelations to us about ourselves. We must protect him so that he does not perish before he has had time to deliver our own soul to us. He must be able to live and become an accomplished artist without sacrificing his talent.

Here, we will address ourselves first of all to that class of alienated Blacks to which we belong, that class which has escaped its environment which is "detribalized." That category is still a minority in Africa, but it is important because it includes the intellectuals and the elite—the ruling class.

That class is the most blameworthy because it is the most enlightened; it is the one which should teach the nonenlightened how a country evolves through the medium of cultural education. Unfortunately, artists hold expositions in vain; ballets and plays, cultural organizations of all types multiply in vain appeals to the elite of the city to amuse itself and instruct itself.

The elite remains deaf. We witness a paradoxical and cruel reality: twenty Blacks out of three hundred answer the call, while ninety out of a hundred Westerners are present at the appointed hour. This is what happens when the show is free. Suppose for a moment that there is a charge; then only Europeans fill the hall. A visitor unfamiliar with the country would think that racial segregation was still in force.

The artist returns home in debt, after having nursed the hope of having a little money from the show.

Enlightened and responsible Africans, do not be astonished if your fellow citizens remain inept at grasping current national realities. How can you correct those who are unwittingly unlightened when you who have the light are even more unlightened?

And then there is African entertainment; it is created to educate all of you. Come with your wife, your children, your mother. You will educate them; you will at the same time provide for the livelihood of the artist who undertakes to speak to your soul . . .

In Dakar I attended the impressive play, "Lat Dior's Last Days." I saw grandmothers, grandfathers, women, children, everybody, perhaps sixty percent of whom were illiterate, jostling, sweating, to buy a dollar ticket to be able to see with their own eyes, even without understanding French, a chapter of their history. It was beautiful to watch the national conscience grow stronger by means of the play, for the negligible sum of a dollar. All Dakar was there, filling the bleachers of Liberty Stadium, a stadium as big as our Stadium of the Revolution. All the Dakarese, in a single national outburst, shared in the play. It reminded me of the theater of antiquity, and I said to myself, "Here is Athens revived."

When will Athens revive among *us*, so that a hundred thousand residents of Brazzaville will be able to give an ovation to our "Koka Mbala's Pot," which was applauded so much at the Dakar festival?

By accepting Black African art as a means of raising our Black and national soul, we will recreate the artist—to use the words of Francis Bebey—we will give new value to his state. We will make him known, we will allow him to perfect his art, we will assure him a prominent place in Black society. In that way we will begin to love and protect art.

For Black art to be loved, it must be restored to its true mission; it must be allowed to assume its primary role.

It must first be assured a suitable place in school programs. Now it has only a secondary role. This was eloquently deplored at the Conference on the Art of the Black World by a UNESCO representative. He characterized education in the arts as one more railroad car on a train that is already too long.

The school should help the people familiarize themselves with Black artists and their works. In this way they will become familiar with themselves, with their own moods, for Negro art is, above all, a way of life. It is not a copy, but a restoration of our nature, as Aimé Césaire said so forcefully. The school should provide appropriate means to help us peruse the art, to establish a dialogue with Black works of art, and hence with our own soul.

The teaching of art should include two stages: It supposes first of all the education of artists. The school should furnish Black artists with means of educating themselves, of perfecting themselves without becoming detribalized. We must avoid the alienation of artists which often occurs in a subtle

and unconscious fashion. An artist may be surprised;
he thought he was expressing an aspect of Black life;
but what in fact shows up is the phantom of a feature
of the civilization that shaped him—often through the
intermediary of a book, a painting, a song, or a
sculpture. We must, therefore, be on our guard, not
just for an hour, but always, so that we resemble no
one but ourselves. For this we must stay as close to
the tribe as possible, while at the same time drawing
inspiration from new methods. We cannot abandon
"tribality." But the school must distinguish, for
Blacks, the idea of *tribality*, from the idea of
tribalism.

Tribality should be understood on the artistic
and cultural level. It is a concept which embraces cultural, spiritual, and educational aspects of the tribe.
According to William Fagg, it designates all that is
Black African and stems from tribal societies. It con-
cerns, therefore, the essence of creative thought and
of authentic sources of life. Tribalism, on the other
hand, refers to all the traits of the tribe that are po-
litically, socially, and economically unacceptable.

The artist must, then, immerse himself in the
midst of the tribe to extract its soul—using the
investigative method of Western Africanists who go
and live with the villagers for years at a time in order
to probe their life.

But it should be remembered that an artist cannot portray what he feels with virtuosity unless he is
himself a virtuoso. From this arises the need for
perfection in his art, whether he be a writer, painter,
sculptor, musician, singer, or dancer. Inclination,

artistic talent, and perfection must blend in the translation of human thought, still more in the translation of Negro thought, which has scarcely begun to trace its course.

The second stage of artistic education is the diffusion of art. I am speaking here of education in reading a work of art, in interpreting it, in analyzing its components—in a word, of esthetic education. A perfect knowledge of Negro art allows the Black African to identify himself with Black society through communication with the soul of that society. It is above all the school that will teach all Black children, not only a privileged few, to appreciate Black works of art and art of other civilizations.

The school should also seek to restore its primary mission to each art. Francis Bebey, attacking the theorists of classical musical education, says we were taught that music was "the art of combining sounds in a manner agreeable to the ear." But that is true only for the West, which no longer has more than an esthetic view of art. The definition is only half true for Black society, which has also a functional conception of art. "Music, for the Black, is the art of expressing life through the medium of sounds, combined or not, agreeable or not."

Bebey's definition translates Black truth accurately. Westerners accustomed to finicky classical music are sometimes disappointed by the cacophony of Black melodies. Still, in my opinion, Bebey is wrong to pay so little attention to harmony. Care must evidently be taken to make sure that Black music expresses life. That is its first mission. But there is nothing wrong in having it expressed in a manner agreeable to the ear. That would give an international value to our songs, since we would be able to reach people particularly sensitive to harmony, who, given a chance, would perhaps be touched by the functional beauty of our songs.

What is true in any case, is that the notion of art for art's sake was once again unequivocally proscribed by the Conference. We have neither time to lose nor effort to waste. We leave the middle-class mind, which always has a superfluity it doesn't know how to handle, to give itself over to art for art's sake. "When the house is burning," a Cambodian literary critic said, "and others are running to put out the fire, only a fool shows his beloved the moon shining peacefully in the sky." "There is a time for everything," says Ecclesiastes, and it is true. There is a time to put out the fire in the burning house and a time to entertain one's fiancee. We hope that in the Black world the time of art for art's sake will be put off indefinitely. In any event, the diffusion of culture, through art, must be brought quickly into the schools. This requires:

a) the inclusion in every level of school curricula of a program of Black African art to compare with the arts of other civilizations, always in the spirit of necessary complementarity.

b) the formation of art education teachers who have a solid basis in history and a deep knowledge of art in the world. It seems to me that three years study beyond high school should be sufficient to prepare acceptable teachers for elementary art education. Careful recruitment should guarantee the final result.

c) paralleling that education and inevitably accelerated at first, Blacks must become involved in research that will reveal as yet unknown facets of Negro art.

d) art education in the schools would be barren without manuals; hence the necessity of preparing easy-to-approach handbooks on art to facilitate teaching reform. In this, governments should take the initiative. But manuals could be dispensed with in the beginning if they could be replaced by permanent expositions of Black cultural productions. What is particularly necessary is that art education benefit from the same consideration as other fields of instruction.

Let it not be said that school programs are already overloaded. I recently saw a reorganization of the schedule at a Brazzaville school which gave certain classes six hours of Russian lessons each week. I have nothing against teaching Russian, but why not give four hours to Russian and two hours to establishing a valid art course?

It is certain that Negro art cannot be loved, and Black life and thought cannot be appreciated to the full by Blacks themselves as long as Black cultural principles are not included in the curricula of Black Africa's schools.

Protection of works of art: A very urgent question presents itself to Blacks responsible for African cultural life: the conservation of works of art.

Black works of art are the physical and material evidence of our spiritual life; they must be protected, saved from destruction, particularly in this African land where rust and mold, to use biblical language, are constantly destroying life. Protection of these works is a necessity all the more urgent because most of them are made of wood.

Unfortunately, there is lack of awareness in this area: we hear convinced nationalists declare in the name of the people and of institutions, "Why spend so much for pieces of wood, paper, and cloth from which we get no material benefit at a time when we are faced with insoluble economic, political, and social problems?"

They have understood nothing, these celebrated nationalists. And we fear that they will never understand anything at all of the problem. Here we have actual degeneration, not only among politicians, but also among the majority of so-called educated Blacks, for whom the cultural life of a developing country is only a negligible aspect of that development. I will give you an example that may shock you: most of Brazzaville's leading citizens, most of the so-called "developed" Congolese of the city, are acquainted with the tiniest bar in the capital and the tiniest football field, but ask them to point out to you the Congolese National Museum, the Congolese art and handicraft factory, the Poto-Poto Art School, the Congolese Research Institute, and they will look at you and shamelessly ask, "Is there a museum in Brazzaville? An art school?"

There are even some who do not know where the French Cultural Center is located—where every week high quality lectures and cultural exhibits on Black Africa are available.

This is really disappointing. And these nationalist and educated Congolese are the true accomplices of the vandalism which emptied nineteenth- and twentieth-century Black Africa of the most representative works of its civilization.

The missionaries came, saying, "Throw that away; it's the devil himself who is dancing in that statue." And the new converts, in the enthusiasm of their faith, heaved everything into the water, into the fire, or into the hands of the missionaries who set up private museums in their own quarters—museums often richer than most of the national African museums.

At the same time, Europeans, Americans, and others, aware of the esthetic value of Black works of art, completed the work of pillage. Actually, it is probable that if missionaries and explorers had not hoarded the evidence of our civilization, it would have long since disappeared, eaten up by the earth, rust, mold, fire, and water. Therefore, speaking objectively, it is better that this evidence of our culture passed into foreign hands and lands rather than remain on its native soil, becoming a formless mass. There it continues to give witness to our life, to excite and amaze other civilizations, while here it would have slept in the night of time.

Nevertheless, and here is the paradox, at a time when all Blacks should work together to save and protect what we have been able to glean and are still gleaning, Black leaders who have the power to furnish the necessary means will slam the door in your face—in the name of the people, of whose aspirations they are often so ignorant.

This is a crime! If you travel from one part of Black Africa to another, you will here and there find large museums and impressive national cultural foundations. In these nations the leaders and the elite have understood that their present draws its meaning only from the past, and that it is the present which prepares the future.

Everywhere else there is total nakedness, spiritual and moral nakedness, and there is a physical absence of cultural life: only little museums timidly set up in creviced hovels.

Leaders, often pushing lack of awareness to the ridiculous, ask themselves if museums should be attached to the ministry of commerce or to the ministry of industry. And they are insulted when a voice of wisdom tells them, even very softly, that a people's culture is its soul, and it cannot and must not be commercialized or industrialized. Many thoughtful Blacks share this opinion. And they can be proud to declare to the world, with Malraux, that the cultural values of a country are not for sale. Others remain oblivious.

Thus, there is a marking of time in the development of Black cultures, a marking of time against which some Blacks try to struggle, the aware men who want to create a working Black African cultural movement so that the Black world may bring its stone to the cultural construction of the modern world—so that it will be not only a consumer of civilizations, to repeat Alioune Diop's idea, but a producer of human values.

That is the business of all Blacks: heads of state, political leaders, intellectuals, artists, religious leaders, mothers of families, young people.

Thoughtful Black Africa is looking for a path for itself. After the savage struggle for political independence, a struggle which convinced the other nations that henceforth Black Africa will have its word to say in the decisions that involve the whole of humanity; a time of silence, quiet, and reflection is in order to allow her to build herself up and to contribute to the building of the modern world.

In the course of this brief introduction to Black African literature, two facts have held our attention. The struggle of Black people for the rehabilitation of their personality, for accession to physical and spiritual independence, was pursued at first on one front: it seemed to be essentially a question of struggle against the invading and dominating foreigner. Black people did not know for a long time that a second front existed and that this front was maintained by Blacks themselves. The Black became a wolf for the Black. Toundi, Samba Diallo and Manuel were all struck down by Blacks unaware of the implications of their actions.

This lack of awareness is one of the most vicious enemies of the Black world. It is an enemy that can be conquered only if thoughtful Blacks learn to unmask and demolish it, not by violence, as certain people advocate, but by serious-minded, human, and creative reeducation. It is time the Black world recognizes that the enemies of a man can indeed be people of his own household. Recognizing this, Black African literature will find a new breath which will allow it to renew itself.